When the Babies Won't Come

Womanhood and Self-worth Defined

To Norma thanks for your support

Sandra J. Pugh

Sandra J Pugh

Love Life !

Dedication

To my mother, Eldora Monroe-Green, who did not give birth to me but loved me completely. Thank you for teaching me about God and his unfailing Love. I will always love you and remember everything you taught me. Most of all, your hard work and dedication as a mother were not in vain. Forever in my heart.
Rest in peace Mama.

To my husband of 23 years, David Elijah Pugh. You are my heartbeat and Knight in Shining Armor. I cannot imagine life without you. Thank you for being the biggest supporter for all of my endeavors. Most of all, thank you for your kind and easy way of just being you. You are the rhythm in my life that keeps me on beat like a Bony James jazz classic. I love you with all that I am.

To my small circle of friends and extended family—Larry Boynton, Delores Jenkins, Janet Healey, Pearlie Kirby, and Carla Wilbert—who love me despite my shortcomings. I thank God for your love and support.

To my babies Danielle McPherson, and Ishamia Turner. Because of you, I know what it feels like to be a mom.

Contents

Acknowledgments

To my Lord and Savior, Jesus Christ, who has done exceeding and abundant things, more than I could ever ask or think. Through the miracle of healing and deliverance from the pain and brokenness that kept me paralyzed and bound for many years, this book is now a reality.

Deepest thanks to my early readers, Janet Healey and Lilly Crook.

To my spiritual leaders, Bishop Ned Adams (rest in power), Pastor Michael Rosier, and Pastors Joel and Patricia Gregory. Whether you provided a listening ear, extended a helping hand, or taught life-changing biblical principles, your dedication to the ministry has been impactful.

To Josh Langston, my editor, thank you for the simplicity of your writing instruction, editing expertise, suggestions, and publishing knowledge, all of which helped to bring this book to completion.

Confusing Childhood

I was your typical little Black country girl living in rural Alabama. With a head full of beautiful, blondish-red hair, and I was one of the biggest tomboys you would ever meet. When I was about four years old, I remember Charlie Green coming to my house from just across the cow pasture where he lived, to see me and tell me that

he was my "real daddy." From what I can remember, Charlie wasn't a bad-looking man. He was a light-skinned Black man of medium height. If I remember correctly, he had a bushy mustache.

He came and sat in a chair in our back yard. "Hi, San, come over here and talk to me," he said.

I said, "I don't want to."

Mama came out of the house and said, "Go on over there and talk to him."

Even though I was a child, I could sense that I was not going to like whatever he had to say. I walked slowly over to where he was sitting in a chair in the yard. He picked me up and sat me on his knee. While I sat on his knee, squirming all around, he started talking to me. "You know that Papa Sam is not your real daddy. I'm your real daddy."

That did not go over well with me at all. How dare him tell me that the man I love so much, who gives me everything I need and want, is not my real daddy! I jumped down from his lap, picked up a handful of rocks, and threw them at him. "You are *not* my daddy!" I shouted. "Papa Sam is my daddy."

My aim must have been pretty good for a small tot, because one of those rocks landed squarely on his head leaving a bloody trail down the side of his face. Mama heard all the commotion and came out to see what was happening.

"Sandra what are you doing?" she asked.

Before I could say a word, Charlie spoke up. "She hit me in the head with rocks!"

"Why would you do that?" demanded Mama.

I looked at her with my big, sad, brown eyes full of tears. Through those tears, I said, "I hit him because he said Daddy is not my real daddy."

And that is how the "daddy baby" saga began, and it went downhill from there.

I suppose you could say I had a unique and confusing family life. From the time I was a baby, I grew up with my biological grandmother, Dora, who I only ever knew as "Mama," and my step-grandfather, Sam, who I only knew as "Daddy." Throughout

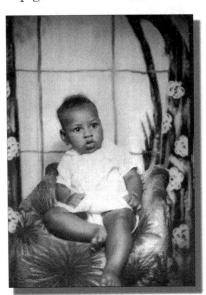

this book I will refer to them as such. They were the only parents I really knew. Having older parents wasn't unheard of, however, their views about life were probably different from the parents of my friends whose parentage wasn't as confusing. Remember, I said my *step-grandfather* was the man I knew as Daddy.

Shall we dig a little deeper? My grandmother brought into the marriage to Sam Green a

2

young daughter named Fannie. Fannie had no biological ties to Sam, and at the young age of 14 she became involved with one of Sam's nephews named Charlie Green. The unthinkable happened; Fannie became pregnant by Charlie at the ripe old age of 14, and at 15 she gave birth to a beautiful baby girl named Sandra. That baby girl was me.

If this sounds confusing, you can imagine how confusing it was for me as a small child. Not only was Sam Green the man I called Daddy, he was both my Step Grandfather and my Great Uncle. I never gave much thought to all of this craziness until I was a teen ager, and bits and pieces of this convoluted mess started to circulate on the gossip circuit.

My mom was a beautiful woman inside and out. She had the most beautiful shapely legs, and when she wore her heels to church, she was stunning. She would not have donned any magazine cover because as lovely as she was, her face was covered with moles or tags as the Dermatologists label them. She never considered having them removed. She often said that removing them could cause cancer.

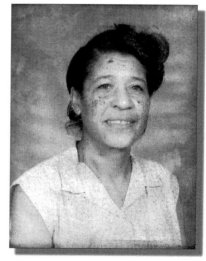

Therefore, she lived out her life knowing that people were staring at her face. She did not let that stop her from having a love of clothes and shoes. She loved dressing for church, putting on her face powder, and fixing her hair.

My mom loved people, and she loved helping people. She would cook and feed anyone in the neighborhood. There was a family friend named Riley who often walked a long distance— approximately twenty miles— from Jacksonville, Alabama to Brutonville, Alabama to visit his niece. Mr. Riley was a very tall, lanky African American man, who my mom knew well. He would stop at our house, about one third of the way on his journey, and stay overnight. Mom would feed him and offer food he could take with him. She believed this was a command from

3

God, and often quoted this bible verse, Hebrews 13:2: "Be not forgetful to entertain strangers, for thereby some have entertained angels unawares."

I acquired my love for shoes and clothes from her. She was a stickler for looking good when you go out of the house. She taught me that I should make sure my hair was done, and my clothes were clean and neat. That is still very important to me now. I don't leave home without combing my hair and wearing makeup and lipstick. Yes, I am a girly girl because of my mama.

Daddy

I can't remember a lot about Sam Green, the man I loved and knew as Daddy. He was a somewhat thin man who had a love for dress hats and stiffly starched overalls. He was very handsome in his own way and had an interesting way of talking to people. I would describe him as charismatic. He enjoyed it when men from the neighborhood would come by just to talk or have a drink. I don't remember a lot about him, because he died when I was 11, but I recall following him around and trying to do whatever he was doing. I suppose one could say for the short time I had him in my life, I was a Daddy's girl.

Once, I went possum hunting with him. I quickly learned this was done at night, because possums are nocturnal. We lived next to an old cemetery, and that is where my dad chose to possum hunt on this particular night. Can you imagine walking through a cemetery at night? Especially since there was no lighting in the rural area where we lived. I was thinking that there was ghost out here, and so I stayed close to my dad.

Daddy brought his hunting dog, Bell. When she found the possum's trail and chased it, the possum would climb into a tree. Suddenly, we heard her distinct bark, and my dad said, "There she goes! She's on his trail." Not long after that we could hear the treetops shaking, and this indicated that the possum had gone higher up into the tree for safety. Once the dog treed the possum, daddy would shine his flashlight directly into the possum's eyes. The possum's eyes were a bright red, and I could see that from the ground. "You see the possum up there in that tree?" he asked.

"I see him Daddy," I said. "What're you going to do now, I asked?"

"We have to get him down from that tree and put him in our sack." He continued to flash that light in the possum's eyes. He said that 'sulled' the possum and explained that meant they were put in a trance-like state.

Then he took out his gun and shot up into the tree near the possum. He did not shoot at the possum, but he scared him so much the possum fell to the ground. Then he grabbed him and put him into his "croaker sack" as they were called back then. It's what we call a burlap bag today.

Once we got home, Daddy put the possum in a pen made of wood and metal fencing. This kept it from escaping. During this time, we fed the possum buttermilk and cornbread.

The Best Barbecue Ever

When I think about my childhood, some fond memories come to mind. One of those is my father barbecuing. The smell of smoked meat wafting through the air would have people coming from all over our neighborhood to get a sample. My dad had a unique system for how he made barbecue. He would dig a hole in the ground about three or four feet deep. Then he would go out into the woods, cut down Hickory trees, and chop them into small sections. He would place the hickory wood in the pit and set in on fire.

When the fire had burned down to just red, glowing embers, he would place a metal screen over the pit, and put the meat on that screen. I can see it now: whole pork shoulders, slabs of fresh ribs, and chicken would all be cooking on there at one time. Mom would be inside making the barbecue sauce, which included her secret ingredients. I was pretty young during this time, but I remember some of the spices that went into that fabulous sauce. Back then, there were very few store-bought sauces, and people made their own from scratch.

Before the meat finished cooking, my Dad would bring the skin from the pork shoulder into the house. Mom would put it in the oven and finish cooking it. Once it was done, we would enjoy eating those crunchy skins, and cracklings sprinkled with salt. Eating pork at that time was not against the "eating healthy" rules. As a matter of fact, it was a staple for most every Black person living in the area. We ate everything on the pig. Folks often said, when it came to eating pork, we ate everything "from the rooter to the tooter." What wonderful times we had when the family got together to enjoy each other. I really miss those times.

Feeling Lonely and Wrong in My Own Skin

The 1960s in Alabama was a time when racial divides were a way of life, and there was much discourse among races in the area where I lived. If trees of every kind, cotton fields, cows, and chickens excite you, then you would have loved my hometown. We entertained ourselves as children running through the fields and swinging on vines in the woods. I wasn't afraid of the animals that could be found in those woods, especially when I was with other children.

Life could also be rather lonely for a little girl, three or four years old growing up without siblings, so I took advantage of every opportunity to spend time with the children living within walking distance. They were the children of James and George Green, who were brothers of Charlie Green, my "Real Daddy." I didn't understand all that was occurring at the time, I just wanted to play with their children.

Between George and James Green, there were 14 children ranging in age. Some were as young as me, and spending time with them was fun. At that time in my innocence, I didn't know this side of my family viewed me in a negative light.

In the winter, I spent most of my days playing in the cotton fields while my cousins worked the fields. Their fathers and my uncles were cotton farmers, and their children were required to work the fields. Back then, children whose parents were farmers could take time out of school and tend to the farming. I just liked the company and became the self-appointed water girl.

Cotton farming was the way of life in the south at the time, and many Black people just picked and chopped the cotton. My birth father's brothers were considered wealthy by all southern terms because they owned their fields. As a result of their wealth, they lived in nice brick homes and drove nice cars.

I remember hastily bringing ice water to my cousins in the summer while they chopped the cotton, splashing it as I went. After they drank all they wanted, I looked for a shady spot to place the cold water. I remember finding some brush one day that looked promising. I stuck my hand under the bush to shade the water jug, but when I pulled it out, it smelled of something that was the worst kind of awful. I had no idea why my hand smelled so bad, but I soon discovered the horrible culprit responsible. One of my cousins said the pungent smell on my hand was left by a skunk.

I went running home through the thicket of brush and briar patches to my mom, crying about the awful smell on my hand. From the look on her face, she clearly did not want to get near me, but what is a mom to do? She soaked my hands in everything she could think of—bleach, vinegar, lemon juice—nothing worked. I walked around with that skunk smell on my hand for a week at least, and washing did not make it go away. The smell just had to wear off on its own. I learned my lesson that day, and I never put my hand in any bushes after that until I had checked them out thoroughly.

We lived in a tiny "shotgun house," which simply means it was one long continuum of three small rooms. We also had a pretty old car. However, just having a car in our community could be seen as a symbol of being well off.

Stomping Grounds

I grew up in a rural area that was pine tree-lined with beautiful, green, flatland parcels throughout. Cottonfields were plentiful, and in the winter, white unpicked cotton lined the fields like fresh fallen snow. Farmland and fields of vegetables and watermelons were equally as plentiful in the summer months. At that time, large chain supermarkets were almost unheard of in the small town where I lived. Most people purchased their vegetables directly from farmers in the area.

Some of the more prominent White farmers had horses and cows. Everyone had gardens with fresh greens and vegetables of all types. One of the vegetables most people grew were tomatoes, and green tomatoes were harvested, too, as they were a popular dish. At that time, people grew vegetables and canned them to make sure they had good vegetables in the winter months. Canning was a process where vegetables were cooked to a certain temperature and put in glass jars with the lids sealed in place.

Right near us were two small towns, Weaver and Lenlock. Not far away were Brutonville and Alexandria, both of which had schools. We had to go into Jacksonville, Alabama, to get our groceries and shop for clothing. Jacksonville State University, a small state school, is also located there.

Jacksonville State University provided employment to many people in the area. I worked there for a short period of time cleaning dorm rooms. The university also provided some of the excitement for the local young people—Friday night dorm parties, and one small watering hole where everybody went to drink beer and socialize.

Bullied Before Bullying Had a Name

Some of the children I spent time with were mean, and today would be considered bullies. Zora, a girl we called Peewee, and James Jr. stand out as the biggest of the bullies. I can remember going to the cotton field where they were working one particular day. I wore a little black hat featuring some forgotten children's character, probably purchased from a yard sale my mom and I had visited. Right away, Peewee started in on me with her ugly words. She snatched my hat off my head and threw it in the dirt, then stomped on it. I started to cry, and some of the older children told her to stop being mean. Then she said, "Oh, I was just playing."

Peewee would ask me questions like "Who's your daddy?" I would say, "Charlie." Of course, Peewee, being about five years older, would come back with something like "Charlie is not your daddy, and you don't know who your daddy is, because your mama is a whore."

This was a lot for a small child to take in. For one thing, I had no idea what a whore was. However, I knew it must not be a good thing because of the way she said the word. As time went on, I naturally learned what it meant.

I would later discover these people saw Fannie Mae as less than them, because of their self-proclaimed status of being "better" than other people. They were the "Black Elite" according to the local cultural norms, because of their fair skin and fine hair texture. I grew up feeling bad about myself, and thought something must be wrong with me. I didn't know that the *something* was the hatred and rejection I had been subjected to at the time. I just knew those people didn't like me or want me in their lives.

This horrible rejection became one of the many events that set the foundation for my life, and created in me a lack of self-esteem that would lead to little or no self-worth. As adults, we must be careful and intentional when we talk to our children, or any child, because they are listening to every word we say. They are also listening to how we say them. Our words have the ability to either empower or tear down.

As I look back and think about those families' self-declared status as elite, I find it really interesting, because not all of those young women in those families were living perfect lives, as people were led to believe. As a child I just looked at the houses they lived in and assumed they must be the ones to take at their word, because after all, they appeared to have everything most of us just dreamed of. I recognize now that I used the image they projected as the measuring stick for my self-esteem, which was being diminished daily by the way they treated me.

I have come to realize these seemingly "perfect" women were also having sex outside of marriage, and some had babies out of wedlock. I discovered their lives were not nearly as perfect as they wanted everyone to believe. Their men were cheating on them, too, and rumor had it that some of their men were living a "down low" lifestyle and regularly having sex with other men.

These acts and the people who committed them were not openly talked about the way my young mother had been. Oh yes, and for those who had the babies out of wedlock, there were still good things said about them. I remember that all we heard was that "Bennie's babies' daddy is such a great guy, and his family is rich and so nice."

Looking back on how things were then, I think I understand some of the mindsets. My take on this manner of thought is this: If you were a part of the right lineage, then you would be seen as pure and perfect in all your ways, and even your indiscretions were seen as just simple little missteps. It did not warrant one in that status of being considered a whore and a slut. No, not by any means, just simply that a perfect girl while in college met a perfect boy and had a perfect little baby. When Donnie, who was the daughter of James Green, was being beaten by her husband, she was just seen as having made a mistake.

As a child, I believed everything that was said about me and about Fannie. I was unable to refute anything they were saying, and didn't have the ability to understand what was happening. Of course, most them were older, and sadly, they were the people with whom I spent a lot of my time.

Despite what they said, I liked these people. Looking back, I think that was the saddest part of all that occurred. Like most children who spend time with other children, I considered them friends, and I wanted them to continue being my friends. I was not about to say anything or try to come to the defense of a woman about whom I knew very little. Although I recognize now, that was not friendship. I think they just tolerated me, especially since they thought so little of the woman who gave birth to me.

In retrospect, as I consider everything that had been said about Fannie, I wonder how could someone so young have become such an awful person and such a well-known whore. In my experience, it takes even the most seasoned whores some time to perfect their trade. Even if she started having sex when she was nine or ten years old, Fannie only had four years to become an expert at her trade. However, these people painted her as a dark figure of a person. The fact that Charlie was a grown man and some ten-plus years older when he impregnated her with a child, was never a factor.

As a child, I wasn't sure what I should conclude about what was said to me about Fannie Mae, but I knew I didn't like how those words made me feel. No one thought to ask me how I felt about what was being said, or if it made me sad or angry. People just went about saying what made *them* feel good or better, or provided them with the laugh of the day.

I know now that those people were heartless and evil. I often ask myself the question how would they feel if someone was saying that to them, or to their small children? I don't think they would like it, but I have discovered that evil has no conscience. The sad fact is that even as adults, these same people are still very judgmental, while spouting some of the most elitist attitudes.

Children are like sponges; they take everything that is said into their small minds and make their own decisions about what it means. When you are a child and reasoning with the mind of a child, and someone is saying horrible things about the people they are connected to, that could make them think they are equally as bad. I have learned there are individuals who need to belittle other people often in order to feel superior.

Based on what I observed and heard, the Green family must have felt superior in some way. Of course, they had all of the attributes of superiority within the Black community where they lived. They were known for looking down their noses on other Black people living in the area. Moreover, they had some of the material items that labeled them as wealthy and elite. They flaunted their material things and thought it granted them automatic rights to judge and mistreat other people in the neighborhood.

I spent and wasted many precious years of my life hating the Green family for their cruel treatment and rejection. With God's perfect love and his help, I have finally forgiven them for their ignorance. I will never again allow how I was treated by them as an innocent child to affect my beautiful life today. Even with the best education that money can buy, some of them still consider themselves to be the superior breed.

The Broken Little Girl Within

There appears to be an unspoken brokenness and disconnectedness within children who are not raised by their biological mothers. I can honestly say I have always felt that I just didn't quite fit in anywhere. The rejection and trauma I endured as a child did not make things any better. I developed into a shy, timid girl, and I had a hard time making friends in school. Everyone else seemed to connect on different levels. Girls would run in packs of sorts, and talk about things they liked. I wanted to be a part of those packs, but for some reason I didn't fit in. I always felt like an outsider, and that feeling remained with me throughout my childhood and into adulthood.

Because I grew up alone, my social skills were limited, and I had no idea what to say when talking to people one-on-one. Watching television offered little if any help back then, because there were no children like me in the shows I watched with whom I could connect. Today, children are involved in all sorts of activities, such as sports and dance. Back then a few girls played softball, but they were the exception to the rule. The rest of us just watched on the sidelines.

My mama grew up in a big family; she was one of seven children. The family is where most children learn great social skills, but hers were limited. Her inability to develop social skills could have had something to do with the fact that she was thrown into an adult role at an early age. She did not have girlfriends to interact with regularly. I am not sure why that was. It may simply have been inconvenience; people's houses were far apart in the country where she grew up.

The only people I know she interacted with were her cousins Knoxie and Pauline. They would talk on the phone, and we would see Knoxie on Sundays, because she lived down the street from Mae Frances, my second cousin, who lived in the urban area of Jacksonville. Those were the fun times, and I loved going to visit her. She had sons who were much older than me, but I still liked seeing them. At one point in my life, Mama's side of the family accepted me and said nice things to me. I could feel the love when I was around them, and it was the one thing that gave me stability during that time. Unfortunately, we did not see them often.

The majority of the people I went to school with all had siblings living in their homes, and they knew how to play cards and other games I was not familiar with. I learned to play Spades, which was a popular card game, when I was a young adult. It was such a fun game, and I really enjoyed playing with David Anderson, the man I married when I was 17 years old, and his family. The only thing I knew previously about playing cards, was that my Daddy gambled, and my mom did not like it.

There wasn't anyone who showed me love often, except for

Mama. The irony of it all, was that I wanted to be liked by the other children. In retrospect, I recognize that social skills are learned through interaction, and when there is limited interaction, one's social skills will be limited. I never learned how to be the life of the party or engage in small talk. Even as an adult, I struggle with what to say when small talk is required. When my husband and I have gatherings at our home, I always try to have some type of entertainment planned. Having entertainment for our guest helps me by not requiring me to make up things to talk about in order to keep my guests entertained.

I Couldn't Wait To Go To School

Growing up as an only child could get really lonely. I could not wait to go to school because I would see the other kids getting on the school bus. They were already going to school and would talk about what happened in school every day. I wanted to know more about what they did, what kind of books they read, and what the teachers said. Where we lived, there weren't any formal activities for children, other than going to church, and that was only on Sunday morning. Otherwise, life was pretty boring. Especially for a smart child like me.

When I was five, I started telling my mom I wanted to go to school with the other children in my neighborhood. Back then, children needed to be six to start first grade. I wasn't sure what actually happened at school, I just knew I wanted to go and be with the other kids. At the beginning of the school year after I turned five, Mom decided she was going to put me on the school bus and send me to school. In those days there were no computers or cell phones, which made gathering information difficult.

I went to school for about six weeks, and my first-grade teacher, Ms. Cunningham, was being pressured by the Principal to ask for my birth certificate. Mom was not about to send the birth certificate because she knew it was not correct. Because of that, I was forced to leave school, and I did not go back until I was six years old. Years later, I discovered why she did not want to send the birth certificate. My name was incorrect on that birth certificate, based on everything I knew. My legal name was Eldora Monroe, which was my grandmother's name.

Evidently, there was some discussion between her and Fannie about what my name would be. Fannie Mae said it was Sandra. However, my grandmother wanted me to be named after her, and she told Dr. Williams, who delivered me, to put that name on the birth certificate. Remember, Fannie Mae was only 15 years old, and apparently Dr. Williams felt it safer to follow her mama's orders.

Womanhood Defined

As a young Black woman living in the south at that time, one's womanhood seemed to be defined by many things, but one clearly defining characteristic appeared to be how many babies a female could produce. I suspect this may have been a learned concept derived from our ancestor's enslavement. Since Black women gave birth to the next generation of slaves, the slave trader encouraged extensive childbearing. Slave owners most certainly encouraged and rewarded this great accomplishment.

I can only imagine what that competition must have looked like and the conversation that ensued. "Did you know that Sadie is pregnant again?"

"Yeah, I heard. You know that's number fifteen for her."

"Master Jones gave her a new blanket and a pair of Miss Jannie's old shoes."

"I only have thirteen kids, but I can beat her having babies."

And so on. I know, this sounds ridiculous, right? Well, guess what? That is exactly what some Black women did then—and still do now.

This gift of childbearing was also a weapon which some women would use to make those who could not have babies feel less than complete, less than being "real" women. Black females have always competed for our Black men. And where I came from, there was always brutal competition for our Black men's affection. When sitting around talking, women would often say horrible things about others who could not have babies. They'd say such things as, "She is not a real woman."

Have you ever been among women having drinks and

conversation? I have, and I have heard women say things like, "I am fertile as a merlin," or "I could have been a breeder as a slave." Knowing that one could give birth was an affirmation of womanhood. With that thought in mind, I had no comments on the subject. Absolutely nothing. As a matter of fact, I refused to participate in those conversations. It would be as if I wasn't even there, and I just wanted to fade into the background.

Why? Because I didn't feel like a whole woman. I saw myself as something far less than a fertile, complete female.

I am by no means suggesting women should not be proud of the fact they are able to produce life. I think they should not only be proud of their fertility, but should also be affirmed and celebrated for carrying a baby and giving birth. However, in my experience, I have seen women use their ability to produce children as a weapon against other women.

In my experience as a Black woman, I have noticed that the competition for the interest of men can sometimes cause women to be cruel. They often choose what they can do in comparison to what another woman can't do, simply to make the other woman look bad. This is a horrible act, and I have seen it crush more than one woman's self-worth. Using the gift that God gives one to hurt another person, is an act that is less than reprehensible. I know now that people who have not learned the art of appreciation for what God gives will use their gift as a weapon of destruction.

Married At 17

After marrying David Anderson at the ripe old age of 17 and not being able to conceive after a while, I didn't know what to do or where to seek help. I tried everything to get pregnant and nothing worked. Early on, I went to the doctor and was told that nothing physically was causing my infertility.

I felt like an empty shell of a woman. There were babies everywhere I went. It was as if someone was playing a cruel trick on me. I would go to the supermarket, and there would be cute babies in every isle. There were babies in strollers at the mall and babies at church. I could not escape seeing babies, which had become the thing that brought me unhappiness instead of joy.

When we would go to the weekly baseball games in Brutonville, there would be pregnant women everywhere. There were women holding newborn babies with toddlers running around all over the ball ground. Just seeing those babies confirmed my inadequacy and shortcoming as a woman, and sent my emotions into a tail spin. I would have done anything to have a baby. As unheard of as it may seem, I was a woman dying due to infertility.

Abused

I don't remember when the beatings actually started; some of those pieces of my memory are a blur. I suppose the pain was so bad, that I repressed some of those memories. I do know exactly when it happened the first time. It occurred one weekend when I confronted him about rumors that he was cheating with multiple women. One of those people was his ex-wife. Of course, he denied everything. "So, where were you all weekend?" I asked.

"I was with my friends," he lied.

"Doing what all weekend?"

"Bitch, you don't question me about what I'm doing," he said.

"So, I'm a bitch now?"

One word led to another, and the arguing intensified until he pushed me, and I pushed back. Well, he didn't like that, and that's when he hit me full force.

David Anderson was a big, tall man, and the blow from that closed-hand punch left me reeling. I could not believe what had occurred, but I knew I didn't want anyone to see my face. I put ice on my eye to help with the pain and swelling. The next morning my eye was bruised and swollen all around. It was a deep purple color I had never seen on anyone's face up close. When he was beating me up back then, it was a horrible situation, and my embarrassment held me captive in that marriage.

I was so heart-broken; all I could think about was how in the world could I have gotten myself into such a mess. I have often pondered, what could I have been thinking to get myself involved with someone like him? Not that I had any real model of what a good

17

man should be. My mind had me justifying that I must have been this whore like Fannie Mae, and of course as a whore and a nobody, my beatings that David Anderson so often doled out were somehow warranted.

My awful life was being gossiped about throughout the family and into the neighborhood. People had a lot to say in the community. One of the people who was talking was James Green Jr., and he should not have opened his mouth, because he kept a woman outside of his marriage for years and years. I knew this woman, and she was really nice by the way. I don't know what she saw in him, but she must have found something to love. Based on my experience with him, I can't imagine what that must have been. James Jr. was then, and is now, just like his daddy—heartless.

According to my mom, James Green Sr. had a reputation in the community for stealing from people in our neighborhood. It was said that he scammed unsuspecting people out of land and homes. He even managed to get his hands on the acre of land where our little house stood for years. He wanted that piece of land desperately and tried to buy it after Daddy died. Mama would not sell it to him, largely because she saw what a scoundrel he really was. She had observed his ruthlessness with other, less-suspecting people, in the community.

When my Dad passed away, James Green called Daddy's grown children by his first wife and tried to get them to give the land to him. They must have agreed to give or sell it to him, because he took it over without even giving Mama the respect of letting her know what he was trying to do. I hated him for what he had done, and the way he had disrespected Mama and treated me all of those years.

I recognize now that he did not go to church, or even pretend to know God. James was greedy and lacked empathy or sympathy for anyone other than his immediate family. Once again, with God's help, I have forgiven him for having been the horrible, mean man that he was. He would be considered a criminal nowadays, most likely for stealing people's home and land.

My life had become a horrible nightmare, and I struggled to find my footing. My faith had wavered, but God gave me the courage

I needed to find my way.

Hierarchy For Men Choosing Women

When I was young and actively in competition for attention and affection, I often wondered why a man would choose to date a woman who had several babies over me when I did not have any children. I thought more babies equaled more responsibility, but apparently that was my reasoning alone. There were a few men who seemed to be able to look beyond that crazy notion and made choices in women based on other characteristics, but because there were so few men, they were taken quickly.

Once, one of my friends, Burrell, told me he loved to date women with lots of babies, because he knew they loved to have sex. Burrell is now deceased. Rest in peace, Burrell. I told him his thinking was awkward at best, because women who don't have a lot of babies also like having sex. Unfortunately, he was not the only man who thought like that.

Additionally, the pool of men for Black women was and is very limited, especially if they desire to date within their own culture. The high incarceration rate among Black males greatly diminishes the pool of available candidates. And then there is the issue of African American men who have decided that African American women are not worthy to date or marry. This can be confirmed, at least anecdotally, by how often African American men who become successful choose women outside of their race.

There are a considerable number of gay, African American men. The men in this "down low" segment of the culture are largely unavailable to African American women due to their sexual preferences. This leaves the few straight men to become a well sought-after commodity, and these men know their value. Even those with no immoral acumen have as many women as they want just waiting in line to get their chance. Many have babies by multiple women, and the women don't seem to mind. Men who are educated and responsible have their pick, and they are not going to marry anyone until they have had a chance to consider as many as they desire.

I suppose that is why I chose the men who simply gave me the time of day, and they usually were the ones looking for someone just like me to take care of them. Or at least, provide them with some type of security they were not capable of providing for themselves. These were the men I was attracted to, and I am not really sure why. It could be they didn't seem to mind that I didn't have or couldn't have babies, or so I thought. That is how it was in the beginning, but of course they always found their way back to their babies' mama or managed to get someone else pregnant.

I was sinking deeper into self-loathing and was unable to recognize anything good about myself. I supposed my desperation for love was showing at all times. The sad thing about the way I felt was that I had no idea what I needed or wanted to make me feel better about myself. I just knew I had been rejected by many of the men I came into contact with, and the self-loathing never went away. It was the driving force behind my life choices. I was scared to death to give myself over completely, because I was sure there were no men who were capable of loving without cheating and/or abusing.

Dressing Up The Outside

I once heard that if you dress up the outside and never clean up the garbage festering on the inside, you are just a "dressed up garbage can." For a long time, that's exactly what I was. I was too afraid to touch that inside stuff. Largely because I didn't know where to begin. The unresolved anger and pain went so deep that it would require chipping away to dig out the root. Just thinking about my past brought tears to my eyes and caused me to feel sadness that would last for days.

Oh, but I learned how to really dress up the outside! I mastered the art of shopping for beautiful clothes and dressing to perfection. I also learned how to wear and apply makeup so perfectly, that professional makeup artists could become envious. I couldn't have babies, but I knew how to work an outfit to make it sing a perfect melody.

I still love beautiful clothes and will walk a country mile for a beautiful pair of pretty shoes. At the top of my bucket list is traveling to Milan, Italy, to shop for shoes. My husband often says that I should have been a personal shopper. My love for clothes and shoes has allowed me to develop great taste in clothing.

In reality, I just have a great eye for fashion, which I credit to my mother and her love for shoes and clothes. Thanks, Mama. Rest in peace; I will never stop remembering and loving you.

I know how to put together an outfit for any occasion. I even do most of my husband's shopping, and he often receives plenty of compliments. Of course, money is always a factor. When God blesses me with as much money as he wants to, my shopping game will rise to the next level.

It has taken a long time for me to be comfortable with being alone, and learning to embrace all of me, even the not so great parts of who I am. Now that I know I am not defined by the clothes or shoes that I wear, wearing beautiful clothes and shoes takes on a whole new meaning. The new meaning is that I *deserve* to have nice things, because my Father owns the "cattle on a thousand hills" (Psalm 50:7).

Recently I started shopping in stores that were a little outside of our budget and was excited to learn how wonderful Italian leather feels and looks on my feet. I have told my husband that if he buys me two pair of really nice shoes a year, I will be satisfied for all special occasions including Christmas. I am making it easy on him.

Real Baby Mama Drama

When I was about 11 years old and living my somewhat happy-go-lucky life, a taxi pulled up in our driveway bearing a woman and three children. My Mom heard the car drive up and walked over to the door. "Who is that?" I asked.

She said, "I don't know, a woman and some kids." As my mom got closer to them, she said, "That's Fannie Mae!"

I was looking at her, and the woman getting out of the car, *and* those kids. I must have looked like a deer staring into headlights. My mind played a tune in rhythm with my heartbeat. Something scary and exciting was happening at the same time.

Suddenly the woman I had thought about on occasion, and wondered what she might look like at times, was getting out of a car right in front of me.

A sense of happiness came over me, because I was seeing my sisters and my little brother for the first time. Fannie Mae came in the house, and she said, "Hey Mama! Hey Sandra! This is Deborah, Sheila, and Willie."

Mama acted as if she didn't know what to do or think. After a moment, she said, "Okay. Well, y'all come on in."

Looking back on this rather uncomfortable time, I can remember that the kids were cute and friendly, but I wasn't sure what to think of them, or Fannie. I just wanted to be close to my grandmother who was the only mother that I had known up to this point in my life. I kept my distance and didn't say much to anybody. I watched from afar, to see what they might do or say. My little 11-year-old mind wasn't sure how to respond to what was occurring. I didn't know if I should hug them, or kiss them, or what.

The next day, the drama began. Fannie was making breakfast and cooking bacon and eggs. She said, "San, you want some breakfast?"

I said, "No, mama is going to fix my breakfast, because I like my bacon really crispy."

She grabbed the bacon she had cooked and crushed it to pieces. "This damn bacon *is* crisp!"

Mama came into the kitchen and asked, "What is going on?"

Fannie said, "She don't want this damn bacon because she said it's not crisp enough."

Mama said, "That's all right. I will make her some bacon."

Things just went downhill from there. There was a lot of arguing and shouting and mean words spoken. This was during the time my Dad was sick and not long before he passed away. Mama was upset with Fannie and wanted her leave because she didn't want her to upset Daddy. I can remember that mama was crying, and Fannie was crying, and I was just confused and sad. Fannie flashed several hundred-dollar bills, and made it seem as if she had it going on in New Orleans.

After a few days of drama, Fannie and those children left, and the next time I saw her I was about 13 years old. Many months had gone by since she came to Alabama, and I was starting to "feel myself" as the old people used to say. I wanted to go see how people were living in the big city. You see, Fannie gave the impression she was living the good life in the big city of New Orleans.

Bus Ride to the Big City

So, early one Monday morning several months later, I got on a Greyhound Bus and rode it all day before getting to Louisiana. I was excited about what was to come and the possibility of living in the big, glamorous city of New Orleans. The ride lasted about 13 hours, and we stopped many times along the way.

I remember stopping in Birmingham, Alabama, and meeting a boy there during that stop. His name was Dwight Mimms, and he was really handsome. We talked a little bit about where we both lived, and I remember him telling me that he lived in Detroit, Michigan. I had no idea where that was, but it sounded exciting. When it was time for us to go our separate ways, we kissed goodbye. That was my first kiss, and it felt... *amazing*. I can't tell you if our breath was fresh or not. All I could think about was that kissing him was great. I thought if this is what the boys are like in the city, I can't wait to get to New Orleans and see more of them.

My dream of what the big city would be like was crushed when Fannie and her man, Junior, picked me up in what is now called a "Hooptie." They were in an old, run-down, blue Cadillac that had a broken door handle on the passenger-side door. I knew then that going to New Orleans was a mistake. Things didn't get any better when we arrived at their house.

I was almost in tears when we drove up to a little shotgun house in one of the worst neighborhoods I could have imagined. My dream of finding happiness in the bright lights of the big city was now totally destroyed. I immediately started to cry and told Fannie Mae I wanted to go home. She called Mama who said, "Send my baby home on the next bus."

Fannie talked me into staying one more day when she mentioned that James Brown was in town and had a concert at one of the local venues. I said I would stay for that show on Tuesday night. I put on the silver lamè suit I had purchased just for this trip. I looked really hot in that white and silver outfit, or so I thought. Thinking back, I doubt I could have looked any more country.

There was a boy named Stanley who lived across the street from Fannie Mae, and he was not bad looking. Stuttering through her words, Fannie Mae called him over to where we were. "Hey, Stanley, this is my daughter, Sandra. She lives with my mama in Alabama."

"Hi, Sandra. You look nice," he said.

"Thanks," I said with my shaky little voice.

He asked, "Where you guys going?"

"We going' to see James Brown," Fannie said.

I was so nervous; I could hardly say anything. But we had a nice time at the concert, and I was thankful Fannie Mae had done that for me.

Back then, I really had nothing with which to compare how Fannie lived, but I knew there had to be something better in the city somewhere. Her lifestyle was nowhere near my vision of what big city life should look like.

On Wednesday, I was back on that Greyhound bus, headed home to my Mama and the life I knew and loved. However, this would not be my last visit to New Orleans seeking something. Even though the experience was not a good one, New Orleans would be in the back of my mind for the rest of my life. I knew there was a place I could escape to if needed, and maybe one day I would return there.

I suppose that even though things were not as I had hoped they would be in New Orleans; it was a part of my experience that I could share with others.

When Love For Family Turns To Hate

Early on in life, before I married my first husband, I felt the love of family. I couldn't wait until Sunday when Mama and I went to New Hope Baptist Church in Jacksonville. I loved going to New Hope Church because I would see everybody I knew there. My cousin Mae Frances and her children would be there. I loved them, and really enjoyed spending time with them. There were five girls and two boys, and I loved being around them.

My cousin Deborah called me "San Man," and I loved that. I always felt wanted and loved when I was with them. Mae Frances's mama's niece was a great cook, and my Mama and I would leave church and go home with them most Sundays. I would see other people in Jacksonville, too, like my uncles Buddy and Leroy.

When I wasn't at Mae Frances's house, I would be at Uncle Buddy's, spending time with my cousin Gloria. I always had lots of fun with her as well. When I spent time with this side of my family, I knew I was loved and liked, and that made me feel so happy.

Shortly after breaking up with my first boyfriend, Billy, I let my cousin Clara wear the little friendship ring he had given me. When I called and tried to get the ring back, she kept putting me off. "San, you said I could have this ring."

"No, I didn't. I said you could wear it for a while." We went back and forth about the ring until she cursed me and hung up. We were never close after that.

When I was about 15, I overheard Mama and Mae Frances having a heated conversation. I came in the house, and Mama was on the phone crying. I asked her what was wrong, but I could barely understand what she said through her tears. I took the phone from her and cursed Mae Frances out.

Clara must have heard that conversation, because one Saturday sometime later when I was at my cousin Gloria's house, she called me and told me to come and get my ring. I went to meet her, and she threw my ring in the weeds. Then she hit me and said I had called her mama a bitch. She and her other sister, Debra, jumped on me and beat me up. My clothes were torn off, and I got all dirty from falling in the grass. That is when my love for my cousins turned to hate.

Being Light Skinned And Pretty Wasn't An Asset For Me

When I was growing up, I didn't have any friends with whom I spent time with on a regular basis. I assumed it was because everyone I went to school with lived far away. Since my Mom didn't drive, I could not get to where the people I knew lived. So, I assumed it was just the distance that made me a loner.

I never thought of myself as being pretty, and I suppose it was because at that time we still lived strictly by society's rule of beauty. That rule? Blonde hair and blue eyes were the ultimate beauty standard. As a Black woman, of course, I would never meet that standard. However, as a Black woman growing up in the south in the 60s and 70s, being a "light skinned" Black girl made me appear more attractive than my darker peers. At least this was the mindset of some Black people.

I suppose this was also the mindset of some of the White people I encountered as well. Having what is considered "Good Hair" was another factor that people thought gave one an advantage. I suppose one could say I had the good hair and the right skin color to give me a leg up in life.

I must have been the only person who didn't see any of this as an advantage. I say that because nobody raced to me to be my friend or hang out with me on a regular basis. I had to find friendship wherever I could, and I never really had that. I assumed there were many other reasons people didn't want to be my friend, and one of those reasons was that something must be wrong with me. I carried that thinking throughout my life. And when I tried to make friends with other women, there was always something that would not allow those friendships to last for long.

Not until recently did the thought come to mind that my good looks and fair skin had anything to do with the distance that other women would put between me and them. The thought wasn't even original. Actually, it came from my good friend, Larry. I told had him about having a hard time making friends in my new state of residence, and he brought up the subject of my good looks. Larry said, "Sandy, you know that's why other women don't want you around their men."

I just laughed. "Why do you say that, Larry?" I asked.

He said, "Because you are a nice-looking woman."

I could not believe what he said to me could be true, because once again I had not even considered the fact that the way I look and dress, even at the age of 62, could be a deterrent for women wanting to be friends with me.

Not long after that conversation, I talked to my friend, Carla, about wanting to move back to Michigan because I was lonely for my life and friends there. Somehow or another we got on the subject of making friends, and Carla said, "You know women won't like you because you are light skinned." I laughed, because I had not considered that to be an issue when it came to making friends. However, I realized I had to give some consideration to what she was saying.

Recently, I contacted Cathy Collins, an old friend of mine I had not been in contact with for years. I knew Cathy when I was growing up, but we weren't really close because she was a few years younger than me. I knew her family well. I had not talked with her in years, since she moved to California some years after I went to Michigan. During our conversation, and out of the clear blue, she said, "San, you were so pretty."

I was shocked to hear this, because it never occurred to me that anyone who knew me when I was growing up, thought I was pretty. I recognize now that the harsh abuse and trauma I was subjected to as a child severely compromised my self-esteem.

We talked for a long time, and she told me she lived in California for twenty or more years and had six children, plus 26 grandchildren. While we talked, I asked her about Gwen, who was her deceased brother's wife. She told me that Gwen had moved from California and was now living in Las Vegas. Cathy gave me Gwen's phone number. When I ended the call with Cathy, I felt genuinely surprised to know that she too thought I was pretty. It almost reduced me to tears.

Gwen was originally from California and had come to Alabama to visit some of her friends. It was there she met Horace Collins, and they eventually got married. Gwen was a free spirit and loved to party on the weekends. I would consider her a "fast" girl by all terms. She loved to drink beer and smoke weed and she even dabbled with speed. I remember her talking about smoking something called "Sherman." I had no idea what Sherman was, but Gwen explained it was a cigar laced with a liquid form of speed. Gwen talked about one of her experiences with Sherman and said, "I was on the dance floor, and I thought I was wearing a long white gown, but in reality, I was wearing, a sweater and jeans."

I recently called Gwen, and we reminisced about old times. I was really happy to reconnect with her. While having our conversation she said, "San, you were beautiful."

I said, "You *really* thought I was beautiful?" And she said yes.

As we continued our conversation, we talked about lots of old memories and some things I had simply forgotten about. I told her the women in Jacksonville hated me, and she again said it was "because you were pretty." These statements, repeated by people I know and respect, amounted to a revelation. More than one person actually thought I was attractive.

When the call ended, I felt sadness, and the tears ran down my face. I thought to myself, it would have been nice if someone had said that, or that I had *any* positive characteristics when I was growing up. I may have seen myself in a much different light, and maybe my self-image and esteem would have been significantly different.

Lack of a Support System

I suppose when there is no support system that confirms your positive characteristics, but only people who highlight all of your negative characteristics, it shapes your thoughts about who you are as a person. I never heard anyone say good things about me; I only heard the bad things. I fully recognize now just how important it is to have positive input in our early years. I say that because even though I have a beautiful voice, I never was confident enough to develop that voice. I still sing whenever given the opportunity amongst friends and family.

Growing up, I did not have any friends I could visit often and play with, because everyone I went to school with lived far away. Of course, there was no public transportation out in the country.

Based on the choices I made, I can see how I internalized all of the negative input I received. When I turned 14, Mama and I started having problems, because I would sneak out on dates, she didn't know anything about. My mom was upset with me all the time, at least that is how I felt. She seemed embarrassed by my behavior. Remember, I was going to be her saving grace and make her feel proud within the community. The funny thing about all of this is that everybody else in the community was doing the same thing.

I took that as confirmation that none of my family cared about me. Of course, I recognize now that people often need to be able to ridicule someone else in order to make themselves feel better, and this was one of those instances.

Feeling Alone And Searching For That Thing

I no longer felt I fit in anywhere, and so the search to find the one thing that could make me feel good about myself was set in motion. I was looking for something that could make me forget that nobody liked or cared for me anymore. And, even though this may not have been the case, it was certainly how I interpreted everything that happened to me at the time. And so, that search went deep and wide.

When I was in my teens and sitting alone, I would have thoughts about who I was as a person. I wasn't sure how to feel, but I knew there must be something very wrong with me if everybody saw something bad in me. I just did not feel complete; something was missing from my life. The sad truth was I didn't have a clue about what I needed to do or be in order to make everybody like me.

In retrospect, I can see that it would not have made any difference. These people had decided something bad about me, and nothing I could do was going to change their opinions. I was on my own to fight the big bad world and learn how to navigate the choppy waters alone. I had been given some great survival tools, and now I would put them to use.

Mama was from the old school about feelings and emotions. She didn't talk about her feelings much. I know she had feelings, because when some of her siblings did something she didn't like, she cursed them out and later had a few drinks as she cried. Needless to say, I learned how to handle my feelings by modeling her. She wasn't wrong or bad, but she was only doing what she knew to do. Clearly, no one had ever told her it was all right to have feelings.

I learned how to drink my feelings away. I recognize now that the drinking only helped temporally, and the feelings came back as soon as I sobered up. Mama taught me resilience. She gave me all she knew about love. She was an amazing woman with a pretty tough exterior. She had never really known love in her life. It had been tough and harsh. When she met and married Sam Green, I can only imagine she was looking for a better life.

Unfortunately, a marriage with 30-plus years of age difference did not get her what she wanted. My mom was subjected to harsh rules by her much older husband. He didn't want her to wear dresses that showed any of her legs, and she had beautiful legs. The marriage provided her a little bit of stability but not the love she deserved or wanted.

I say that because I never observed them showing any affection at all. I just remember they argued a lot, about one thing or another. There was never any violence, but looking back, it was clear they just did not appear to be the happiest couple. I suppose when you come from absolutely nothing, just having food and clothes could feel like so much more.

My mom wasn't a gentle, cuddly woman, and I was fully grown when we started saying I love you to each other. I suppose I learned how to settle for less, or maybe not even know what to demand from her life story. Somehow, I just knew she loved me. I felt it in my spirit and my heart.

Her family were share croppers on a place called the Crow Farm. The Crow family was a wealthy White family who owned land and businesses in town. I remember that mama had one of Mr. Marx' pictures in her things. It is my understanding Mr. Marx and his family once owned Crow farm. Unfortunately, I don't know what happened to that picture.

Thinking about how things were back when my Mom was a child makes me sad and angry. I know she did not have any of the opportunities her White counterparts benefited from. Mama only had a sixth-grade education. You would not have known that talking to her, because she was so smart and crafty.

My Mom gave all that she had been given, and she had a heart of gold. Sometimes, she could come across as being really mean, but everyone who knew her loved her. She was a great cook and made some of the best homemade biscuits anyone ever wanted to eat. I suppose I could sense her sadness, and I wanted to make her life better, but I didn't know how to make that happen.

What We Did For Fun

Country life had very little to offer in the way of entertainment. I recall going to a small building in the woods called the Lonely Pines—a small place with very rustic booths and chairs, a small kitchen, and an even smaller dance floor and stage. I wasn't driving then, and I relied on my older cousin Gloria Anne who we sometimes called Duke for transportation, because my uncle allowed her to drive his car sometimes. Of course, we had to make sure of his drunken state before we asked to take the car, and even then, he would make us beg.

When we went to the Lonely Pines, I thought I had gone to Hollywood. I suppose it may have been because of the clothes some of the people wore. People were dressed "to the 9s" as we would say. Many from the community were there, including a few guys and others I had never seen. This became a regular hangout for me on the weekends.

When I wasn't at the Lonely Pines, I was at one of the other little spots. We also had a juke joint called Lint's. Lint was short for Valint, who happened to be one of my friend's aunts, and she ran her juke joint in a house. It was a small, white-framed house which sat on a dark, unlit road in Brutonville, Alabama. The house had been renovated into one big room and a small kitchen area. On Friday nights, everybody who was anybody went to Lint's place. The music being played by the band was loud, and people were engaged in conversation all around. Laughter filled the air, and the smell of chicken frying was very familiar.

All of the other little hole in the wall party spots were further away, and without transportation, getting there meant being reliant on others who had cars.

One could buy beer and liquor at the Lonely Pines, and it was just what I needed because of all the people I hated and didn't want anything else to do with. I had not learned how to forgive, or how to process disappointment. So, I just held onto all the feelings of hate and disappointment for many years. I thought everybody hated me for one reason or another.

I had no idea that disagreements could be resolved, because no one appeared to be interested in resolving them with me. I assumed that once you had a fight or an argument, those people were done with you. This was not an entirely incorrect concept, because sadly, most people where I came from did not stay friends after arguments and fights.

How I Met Billy

Earlier, I mentioned "Peewee" who was actually my older cousin, Zora. I think of her as the meanest one. She had a car, and when she needed someone to keep her company, she would let me ride with her to Anniston on occasion. Anniston was about twenty-five miles from Jacksonville, and it was considered the "city." Zora would go down there to visit our grandmother whom we all affectionately called "Mom Mary." Once there, we would go around the corner to visit Zora's boyfriend, Jimmy.

Once while we were visiting him, I met his friend, Billy. A short and stilted conversation followed.

"Hi! I'm Billy. What's your name?"

"Sandra."

"So, you're Zora's cousin?"

"Yes."

My one-word answers should have told him I was immature. It must not have because we exchanged phone numbers, and he started calling me. Looking back, I realize Billy was not cute at all, and his teeth were in need of a really good brushing. He started calling me and talking about going out, but I knew Mama would not allow it since I was only 14 years old.

But that didn't stop me. I wanted to spend time with Billy, and so I agreed to go out with him. Of course, I did not mention anything to my mother. When he and his friend showed up, I just ran out and got in their car, while shouting out something like, "I'll be back in a little while." I am not sure if she ever knew I was going out with a boy.

First Sexual Experience

As we were riding along and talking, Billy made it very clear he wanted to have sex, and of course, I didn't know what to say or do. We were riding in the back seat of the car with his friend as the driver. Billy told his friend to pull into a remote area and park. His friend stopped and got out of the car.

Then Billy started kissing me, and I remember him saying something like, "Okay, baby, you ready?"

"Ready to do what?"

"You know! Make love."

"I don't know, Billy. I've never done it before."

"Well, you just relax and let me show you what to do."

I was scared to death and relaxing wasn't going to happen, but I wanted to experience sex because, of course, it would make me become a woman, or so I thought. Even more than that, I wanted to be loved. I thought doing what he wanted would make that happen.

I remember Billy saying something like, "I promise I'll be careful."

I experienced some really interesting feelings when we kissed, and I wanted more of that good feeling. And this connection thorough sex appeared to be the thing that would give me what I needed to feel complete.

As I considered trying the sex thing, I had many thoughts about what it might be like. Would it hurt? What should I do afterward? Even though I did not say no, I was terrified. When he attempted to put his penis inside me, I clamped my legs close together. I don't think he ever actually made it inside of me. However, just having someone want to have sex with me made me feel wanted. After the incident with Billy, I remember standing in the mirror looking at myself, and thinking I am a woman now.

Even though my first experience at sex was botched at best, it made me feel wanted by someone. It was a feeling I had never experienced, and I wanted to feel that way more and more. It seemed clear, sex would be the thing that would get it for me.

When the night for my second date with Billy rolled around, we double-dated with his friend and his friend's girl. Billy wanted to try the sex thing again, but I was still terrified.

The girl with Billy's friend kept saying, "Make sure you take a douche." I had no idea what a douche was, and I was certainly not going to ask my mother. The girl told me I should check around the house for a "douche bag" when I got home. I looked all over for it and finally found it in my mother's clothes closet where Mama kept it hidden away.

During this time, I discovered that douching was very important, and knowing what type of douche powder to purchase and use was equally as important. I remember that Massengil Douche Powder was the most popular brand of douche product at that time.

There were no pictures or books or Internet to access for directions, and I fumbled through it horribly. It was very awkward trying to figure this process out without assistance, but I wasn't about to ask Mama!

Underinformed About Sex From The Beginning

In our home, there were no conversations about boys, or sex, or the difference in the anatomy of males and females. Mama said, "look at the man's shoes," and that will tell you what kind of man he is. And, like most children I suppose, I had no idea where babies came from. As a child, I enjoyed playing with dolls, because that is how little girls are programmed. Back then, television commercials about toys for girls featured some type of doll or kitchen appliance, which had all little girls begging their parents to buy those toys for them.

As females, we are wired internally to be care-givers and nurturers, and maybe that is why everything in our society points young women toward motherhood. In some African cultures, womanhood is determined by the age a young woman gives birth to her first child, and the hierarchy of female prominence is determined by the number of times she gives birth. However, as a young child, thinking about where actual babies came from never entered my mind. When I became a teenager, I quickly learned how this one aspect of femaleness was viewed in my neck of the woods. Which leads me to the topic of sex education, or the lack thereof.

I often look back and reflect on how I received my information about sex and how women become pregnant. For a girl growing up in rural Alabama in the late 60s, sex education came in the form of a romance magazine. I don't remember ever having a real conversation with anyone about sex when I was a young girl. I had no idea what actually took place when a man and women engaged in sex. I vaguely remember hearing my mother say to one of the other women in our neighborhood, "You know Bertha broke her leg." I also heard rumors such as "I heard she has a bun in the oven." I had no idea these terms were code for a woman being pregnant.

No one ever explained how the sperm and the egg connected during sex, not even in school. Back in the early 1960s sex was not openly discussed. At least not where I grew up. Sex was mentioned in "code" and whispers or occasionally at some place like the juke joint. For those of you who may not be familiar with this term. The Juke Joint was a place that people went to buy shots of alcohol and listen to the music being played on a Juke Box.

You may wonder what a jukebox is. They are large pieces of equipment filled with 45-rpm records that one could play for a charge of twenty-five cents. Simply insert a quarter, make a selection and the music would be played. Of course, if several people made selections before you, then you had to wait to hear your tune played.

Even the information I received about starting my menstrual cycle was sketchy at best. Thinking back, I must have been about 11 years old when my grandmother, who was my sole parenting figure and the only mother I knew growing up, had a very short conversation about getting my period. I vaguely remember her saying something like, "You know you are becoming a woman, right?" And I said yes, but in reality, I didn't have a clue about what would actually happen when my menstrual cycle started or how I would care for myself.

I recall the day I started my period. Mama and I were at the White woman's home where Mama worked as a housekeeper. I went into the bathroom and discovered blood in my panties, and I put Vaseline on my vagina and stuffed my under-wear with toilet paper. I thought to myself, God this feels really weird, and I don't know if I should tell Mama. And I didn't until later that night.

Not only did we live in the country, but since my father's death a few years earlier, we no longer had transportation. During that time, the stores all closed very early. When I finally got up the nerve to tell my mother I was bleeding, it was too late to get to the store to buy pads. She made me some substitute pads from old sheets, and the next day we went and bought sanitary napkins.

Buying pads was an interesting learning experience, because there were many different brands, and at that time they all required a belt to hold them in place. I distinctly remember a big bulge in my clothes that could not be hidden. The pad felt awful between my legs, and I wanted to make sure no one could see it through my clothes. So, for the rest of the day while at school, I constantly checked and re-checked my clothing.

Men must have created those pads, because a woman certainly would not have designed something so bulky and uncomfortable. I eventually learned how to wear them and adjust them so they remained unnoticed.

Cultural Beliefs And Myths About Menstrual Cycles

As a young African American woman growing up in the rural south in the early 1970s, there were many different beliefs and myths in my culture about what should and should not take place during the menstrual cycle. For example, I heard one should not take a bath during a period or drink cold water, and by all means, don't eat watermelon.

Now I know none of these things had any scientific basis for negative effects on a woman's health during their period. In spite of all the nonsensical "common knowledge," I did pretty much everything I was told not to do. However, I am sure there was some valuable information I did not receive, because not many women spoke openly about their periods during that time. Now all the information a young girl needs is provided either on television, in school, through friends, or on the Internet.

Birth Control

Like everything else related to sex and pregnancy, I had not been informed about birth control pills, and back then people were not talking about it as much as now. I knew nothing about condoms or where to buy them. And of course, unlike today, there were no television advertisements or billboards marketing them. Shirley Ann, an older family friend known for her promiscuity, gave me my one and only lesson about birth control.

I really liked Shirley Ann because she would talk to me about things my mom would not dare discuss. I told Shirley I was seeing this boy and was having sex with him. She said I should go and get some birth control pills.

"I can't go, Shirley, because I'm too young, and mama won't approve it for me."

"Well," she said, "I have lots of pills, and I will give you some." She gave me several packs, and I started to take them, but obviously they were too strong for me, because my breastsquickly became swollen and tender to the touch.

I never really thought about getting pregnant and what that would mean for me, but at times I did think having a baby would give me someone to love of my very own. Once, the boy who was asking me to have sex mentioned condoms, which was something I wasn't familiar with. The ones he purchased were ribbed, and they were painful. After that experience, I didn't ask anyone else to use them. You see, another important piece of information I had not received concerned sexually transmitted diseases or STDs. I didn't know they existed or what the consequences were.

So, the next man I had sex with, who I will call June, didn't even ask about using condoms, and I ended up with an STD. Later, he told me he had one and that I should go to the doctor and get myself checked out. I was so stupid; I did just what he told me to do. The doctor gave me penicillin, and I took all of it. When I again spoke to the man who'd infected me, he said I had to go back to the doctor and make sure that I was cured, and like an idiot, I did just that. The doctor said I was fine.

Looking For Love In All The Wrong Places

As time went on, I met the person who would become my first husband, and at seventeen I thought I had found my soul mate. David was tall, handsome, and very popular. He was the best dancer around. I can see him now, tall and lanky as his body glided across the floor, dipping and flexing. When he finished his dance moves, everybody clapped. I was really interested in this young man, but there was just one problem: his soon to be ex-wife, Ora Ann. She was always lurking around and letting it be known the divorce was not yet final.

One night while I was at Lint's place having a few drinks and looking for David Anderson, Ora Ann got in my face. "So, you the bitch fucking with my husband?"

"I am not a bitch, and you don't want to fool with me," I said.

I heard rumors that she was coming for me, and I had been scared of what might happen if we ran into each other. At some point all my fear left me, and I went into defense mode like a warrior preparing for battle. So, on this night I took my Mama's pocket knife with me when I went to Lint's. I had the knife open in my bra, and when she got close to me, I pulled it out and started swinging it at her. I could feel the knife connect to her arms as she let out a scream.

After this incident, which was crazy at best, I felt empowered. At least people knew I was not a push over. In some small way it gave me the respect I was looking for. I could hold my head up now because I had proved myself based on mindsets in my culture about defending your honor.

I now understand this is how people end up committing heinous criminal acts in our society. Someone gets called a name, and their friends or peers encourage them to retaliate by saying things like, "You going to let them get away with that?" Then the person feels compelled to get even. God was looking out for me, because this 'beef' did not end tragically.

In retrospect, I imagine she was fighting to maintain her status as the wife, and I was fighting for reasons that were not clear. Meanwhile, the person who caused all of this unrest was gaining status. His maleness was placed on a platform for other women to view.

The mindset seemed to be, if he was being fought over, then he must really "have it going on." In other words, he must be great in bed or maybe he gives his women gifts, or something else to be desired by other women. However, for me he had never been any of those things. As a young woman with little experience with sex, I had little with which to gauge his sexual prowess.

I just wanted to be loved by someone. Little did I know that I was seeking that love from someone who didn't have a clue about what a healthy relationship even looked like. He had not had a good model of love in his home, either. His father worked and tried to provide a living for his wife and children, but his mother was, by definition, a rather loose woman. It was rumored that she was involved with a man in the community. While crying about how David was treating me, she said if I thought he was cheating with other women, I should find myself another man to get involved with. She went on to say that she had a friend, and I figured out the rest.

I wanted someone desperately because I knew women were also defined by whether or not they had a man, and David was the person I desired at that time. After the fight with his wife, I could not back away from him. So, I continued in that crazy relationship and followed through with marriage. The sad part about it was that once I got into the marriage, it turned bad, and I did not get anything that I wanted. As a matter of fact, I was even more miserable than I was when single.

Discovering Infertility

Barren is a term found in the bible. It applied to women who were unable to have children. You may remember Hannah, and her inability to give birth. She talked about how the other women looked at her and treated her. She expressed her feelings of inadequacy and worthlessness. Hanna expressed that she felt disgraced by her inability to have babies. In my inability to conceive, I acquired the label of being barren. I guess one might say, I earned it.

I wore that title like the "Red Badge of Honor" and demonstrated it in all my behavior. Depression wrapped around me like a wet blanket I could not shake loose. And so, there was one more thing resonating in my spirit which told me I was not just barren, a term that made me cringe, but I was also not a "Real Woman." The sad part of this is that I had not been tested by a professional to determine what the problem was. Not until I moved to Michigan many years later, did I get an official diagnosis.

Because of my inability to conceive, I never felt I could compete for the "Good Men." Of course, as I think about it, I am not even sure if I ever knew what good men were. No one had ever sat me down and said, "Daughter, a good man should respect you, and protect you, and provide for you." All I ever knew was that men served a purpose, and I knew I wanted a part of that. I was so desperate for love, that I accepted the first man who came along.

Remember, I was once a shy little thing, and I didn't have the nerve to walk over and talk to guys. Even when I was drinking, I had to have a few to feel good enough and have the nerve to say anything to a guy. Although my recollection of having sex as a young girl has faded, I remember there wasn't much talking before we actually got down to business. Going straight to sex meant avoiding a lot of talking. This made things even more awkward, because once the sex was over, I had no idea what to say. Of course, the guy was young and rather inexperienced as well, and had even less to say.

My Mama Stood Up For Me

The day after my fight with Ora Ann, her mother, Jewell, called my Mama and told her about it. I had already told Mama everything, and she got really mad. I could hear the conversation she was having with Jewell.

"Jewell, I hear what you are saying, and didn't Ora Ann know she was pregnant when she got in Sandra's face? Well, she put herself in that position. I tell you what, nobody better hurt *my* baby, or they will have to deal with me. And you don't want that!"

I was so proud of Mama taking up for me. Unfortunately, her love wasn't enough to spare me from all the misery that was coming on a fast train.

I Won?

I wanted David Anderson to be my man and give me the love I so desperately needed, and I did everything I could to get him. I went into that marriage without any solid information; desperation was my motivation. I needed my mother's signature to get married, because I was only seventeen years old. She did not want to do it, but I told her I was leaving anyway. With that, said she went ahead and signed, allowing me to get married. Though I was elated, I know she probably blamed herself when the marriage went horribly wrong.

My feeling of elation did not last for very long, because he was unfaithful from the very beginning, and abusive, too. I certainly did not find what I was looking for and in need of—affection, care, and concern. The abuse happened more and more, and then embarrassment began to set in. Above and beyond my need for medical attention, and counseling, I prayed no one would find out.

The abuse wasn't just an occasional smack; it was severe from the beginning. He would beat me with his fist, knock me down, and kick me. I clearly remember my first black eye; it was during my senior year in high school. I hardly ever wore makeup at that time, but I had to put it on so I could pose for my graduation picture. I hurt both emotionally and physically, and I was embarrassed about how I was being treated. I knew no one would come to my rescue. I didn't have any friends.

In retrospect, I realize that being pretty and "light skinned" was a recipe for making other girls avoid me and shun friendship. They must have thought I would steal their men or make them look bad. I felt sorry for myself and drank to try to feel better about what was happening to me. I spent a lot of time by myself, feeling lonelier as time went on.

I certainly did not find any friendship with David Anderson's family. His mother hated me from the beginning, and his sister did as well. I felt the aloneness deep within, a feeling that made me want to die. At that time Black people did not commit suicide at the rate they do now. A survivor instinct lived within me, and it was the thing that kept me from killing myself.

I had a small circle of people in my life, and one might think a young girl would have someone she could call on to come to her rescue, but I could not think of a single person who would come to see about me without judging me or talking about me like I was a dog. I knew not to call my Mama but not because she didn't love me. I just did not want to bring any more disgrace on her. She had gone through that with Fannie Mae, and I felt deeply concerned about adding to her disgrace. And even though I didn't call or tell her what was going on, I knew she was the only lifeline I had. Still, my embarrassment would not allow me go home to her. At least not until. I realized I could not take any more of the misery and abuse.

More Embarrassment

One of my teachers came to me during class and told me that Mr. Montgomery wanted to see me in his office. I was scared to death. What could Mr. Montgomery want? I walked into his office, and he started to talk to me about my black eyes. "Sandra, people have noticed you have had black eyes and bruising. Do you want to talk about it?"

"Well, I am trying to finish school, and then I am going to get myself out of the situation."

That's when he told me he knew George Green. I asked him not to say anything to him about the situation, but I am pretty sure he had already mentioned it.

The one thing I remember most about all of that abuse is the one incident when he cut me with a knife on my arm and my back. This was because of an argument we had about his cheating with other women.

"You're cheating with that bitch Eve," I said.

"You're crazy," he said, "You don't know what you're talking about."

One thing led to another, and before I knew it, he had knocked me down.

Normally, he would then apologize and ask me to forgive him, and I would. Like most abused women, we look at the good part of our abuser. I was no different. I fell in love with a charismatic man who was loved by a lot of people. I wanted to pretend that none of this was really happening to me. I did not have a clue that this was wrong and needed to stop. As hard as it might be to believe, I managed to graduate.

The White Doctor Was A Pervert

Despite the fact that I was being beaten on a regular basis, I still wanted to work and be productive. I suppose my mom taught me through her demonstration that hard work was a good thing.

After I graduated from high school, I started looking for a job. During this time, using the local Unemployment Office was a good resource. In spite of the fact I had my high school education, I was referred for a house keeping job. In the late 1970s, a high school education was a great accomplishment. However, as a young Black woman living in the south, making use of it was a challenge.

The job was supposed to be on an Army Depot nearby. I received a call from the person who claimed to want to hire a house keeper. We agreed that he would pick me up so I could come and see where I would be working.

When he arrived to pick me up, I was surprised to see that he was a middle aged white man. He was dressed in a suit, and appeared to be a professional. I was fooled by his appearance. Once we got to his home, he showed me around the house. When we got to the bedroom, I noticed there were women's clothes in the closet. I asked him if his wife would be home soon, and he said that his wife had died recently.

I started to feel uncomfortable at that point, but I was young and inexperienced. I had no idea what a real interview was supposed to entail, and so I went along with what he was doing. At some point he said that if I was going to work for him, he needed to draw blood, and I thought how odd that was. I should have left then, but I was scared and did not have a ride.

I listened to his spiel, and then he started to talk about having sex. I knew Black girls who slept with White men for money, and I was considering doing it. I had started taking my clothes off when I

46

changed my mind. Of course, he was upset with me and begged me not to tell the people at the Unemployment Office about what happened.

This was in the late 1970s, and who was going to believe me over a White man anyway? I felt like a fool for allowing this to happen. I didn't say anything to my crazy abusive husband, who would only have accused me of encouraging the man to do what he did. This was a secret I thought I would take to my grave.

It was a while before I went back to the Unemployment Office, and I managed to conjure up enough courage to tell them some of what happened. I said that he did not want a housekeeper but a girlfriend. The White woman I spoke to said she had heard that from other people, too.

Today he could be arrested for soliciting sex, but back then and especially in the deep south, he got away with harassing young women like me for what he wanted. I learned a valuable lesson that day about men who take advantage of inexperienced girls. My Guardian Angel must have been watching over me, because that experience could have gone differently and much worse. I could have been raped or even killed.

Financially, I didn't have anything, and David wasn't working. That was the norm for him. I was desperate, because I wanted to progress in spite of the abuse I endured. I became employed after that and worked every day. I was always a very hard worker, and my employers really liked me.

Unfortunately, all of the work was physical labor. For example, the first job I had after high school, I worked with Ms. Virginia at the Budweiser beer warehouse in Anniston as a beer stamper. Back then beer was stamped manually, one can at a time. I learned to do that job quickly and rather enjoyed doing the work.

Desperately Wanting To Get Pregnant

All the women around were having babies, and that was all that I could think about, but no matter how hard I tried I wasn't getting pregnant. Women would say things like "Just relax," and it will happen. Or they would say "Try getting on birth control and then get off," but nothing worked. I just could not get pregnant, and

I wanted it more than anything. No matter how beautiful or smart I was, nothing could or would, in my opinion, define my womanhood like having a baby. I also wanted a baby because I would have someone of my own who would love me unconditionally.

It never occurred to me that being beaten and cursed and cheated regularly could stress me out, and affect my ability to get pregnant. I just thought something was terribly wrong with me. This was one more defeating aspect of my life that caused me to retreat further into isolation.

There was no one for me to talk with about how I was feeling, and nobody went to a therapist at that time, at least not any Black people. Some people went to a pastor or priest, but most just suffered in silence. I had not even been introduced to the idea of going to therapy. I couldn't even bring myself to talk to my mama about how I felt. I just drank and sank deeper into depression. I allowed myself to be abused possibly because I felt empty and useless.

Baby Mama Drama

To add to my defeated spirit, David Anderson's ex-wife would show up often and stay with his mother. Ms. Ex would stroll into town with her two babies and be crowned the queen bee for a weekend by his mother and family. Ms. Virginia really loved those grandbabies, and she had always liked his ex-wife. I suppose they had a lot in common. His ex knew how to play the game, and she had a man on the side to fill her empty hours.

Ms. Virginia didn't have much for me, because for some reason she thought her husband had fathered me. Apparently, rumor had it that Robert Anderson and my birth mother had been involved at one point. She made it painfully clear she did not want any part of me.

Her idea that I was Robert Anderson's child was proven wrong when it was confirmed that Robert and Fannie Mae were never sexually involved. This meant I could not be his child, but by then the emotional damage had been done. This had been one more battle I had to fight and fight alone. I hated everything about that marriage, his mother, and his sister, but I was so desperate for love that I stayed there and continued to be abused for almost three years.

Black And Blue And Beaten Beyond Recognition

David would go out and get drunk or high, and when he returned, he would find a reason to jump on me and beat me up. My mom didn't know what was happening at first, because I would stay away from her until the bruises and black eyes healed. I did everything to try and cover up the black eyes, but nothing worked. When I was beaten beyond recognition once again, I found my way home to my mother's house.

Things were bad, and my face was black and blue; my eyes were almost swollen shut. I remember the cuts on my back being so bad I was sure I needed stiches. I had heard that the hospitals and police did not give any consideration to Black women who were abused. For that reason, I would not go to the doctor; I was too embarrassed.

How horrible to live in that kind of abuse, and not care enough about yourself to go to the doctor. Maybe that is why I now go to the doctor for everything. I know the embarrassment of abuse can make the victim feel ashamed, and that shame will remain with them throughout their life. Shame is a way of abusing one's self without knowing what is happening. I hated the life I created for myself, and all I knew was that I was hurting and sad and lonely, but I had no idea how to get better.

Going Home For Good

It was a Friday night, and David Anderson already had his plans for his usual weekend routine, which was to leave home on Friday and come back on Sunday. It must have been God at work in my life, and me finally listening to his instructions, because I would usually just spend the weekend alone waiting on him to come back. That day was different, and I could feel it. After work I went home and started to cook dinner. I asked him if he wanted some pork chops, and he said he did. I put those pork chops in the skillet and started cooking them.

I knew David was going out soon, as he usually did. He said he was going to meet up with his friends. I had a plan, which was to leave and go to my Mama's house.

"Can you watch these pork chops while I go get some beer?" I asked.

"Yeah. I got it," he said.

I jumped in that car and drove as fast as I could into a future free of David Anderson and the abusive life, I had lived for the more than three years.

As I drove along, many different thoughts ran through my mind. Where would I live, and how would I survive? What would people think of the mess I had gotten myself into, especially among the people I knew in Jacksonville. Those were some of the most judgmental people around. I didn't know what I was going to do with my life; I just knew I needed to leave, and so I did.

Once again, I went home to my mother seeking refuge. I am sure she did not believe I was done with my marriage, because I had been at this juncture many times before.

"Well, Sandra, how long are you going to be here this time?" my mother asked.

"I'm here for good mama," I said, "and I am never going back."

I know she did not believe me, but I meant every word. I felt lower than dirt, because my mother had to endure all of that foolishness. I wanted my life to be better and to redeem myself with my mother and anyone who would give me the time of day. Before long, I started to feel I needed a change of scenery.

Fort McClellan, Military Base

After I left David Anderson, I settled into being single, but I was young and lonely, and I was on a mission to find a boyfriend. I started hanging out at Fort McClellan, the military base in my home town. Fort McClellan was not only a military base, it also provided entertainment for our small rural area. Prior to my break up with David, I had not been on post and was not familiar with what really happened there.

I went there with my cousin Linda, and we went to the NCO Club. It was a small club that sold drinks in glasses, which was different for me. Most of the small clubs or "holes in the Walls" where I was from served a shot in a paper cup. The NCO Club was clean and had tables and a DJ. The NCO Club also served mixed drinks which was really nice. Linda liked going to the Officer's club on the Fort McClellan base, because she believed people who went there were more mature.

My friends and I spent a lot of time at Fort McClellan, and I was sure I would find a man there. Unfortunately, after a year of going to clubs on the military base, I still wasn't seeing anyone regularly. I would have settled for a relationship that was strictly sexual, but the competition from the other young women in Anniston was fierce. I often saw a girl named Ivey whom I thought was confident and beautiful, and she would always be in conversation with one of the soldiers residing on post.

I on the other hand, was shy and waited on the guys to say something to me, because I did not feel confident enough to approach them. I was the wall flower who just vanished into the darkness. I did not really know how to do all of the current dances and when a guy would ask me to dance, I would be so nervous that I longed for the moment when the song ended.

I remember going to the 123 Club at Fort McClellan one night with my friends. I soon discovered the Club was intended for the young soldiers in boot camp. Clearly, all the young women in Anniston must have known this as well. That night just happened to be a night when the soldiers were returning from basic training. The place was packed with horny young guys, and I thought I had died and gone to heaven. You could hardly turn around without bumping into someone, and it was so much fun. There were guys in green military uniforms everywhere. I gave my phone number out to a lot of them, but nobody called.

A Fresh Start

"Perhaps travel cannot prevent bigotry, but by demonstrating that all peoples cry, laugh, eat, worry, and die, it can introduce the idea that if we try and understand each other, we may even become friends." —Maya Angelou

As time went by, I decided I needed a change, and the opportunity arose when my cousin Brenda, Mae Frances' oldest daughter with whom I grew up in Alabama, came home from Detroit to visit. I decided at that moment that I would move to Michigan.

"Brenda," I said, with a note of determination in my voice, "I want to move to Michigan."

"*You* want to move to Michigan?" she asked with a puzzled look on her face.

"Yes, I do. I need a change of scenery. Can you ask your husband if I can come and stay with you until I find a job?"

It wasn't long before she informed me that I could come and stay with them.

I had only traveled twice, once to New Orleans and once to Atlanta, Georgia, to visit Six Flags amusement park. I packed my bags and left behind all of the pain and misery I had experienced in Alabama, or so I thought. I got on a plane for the first time in my life; it was exhilarating. The plane that flew from Oxford, Alabama, was small and bounced around with every wind that came. I didn't know what to expect about the plane that would later take me to Detroit. I just knew I wanted to get there.

I went to Michigan scared but excited about getting a fresh start. The place was so different. It was a city with neighborhoods and subdivisions. The houses were much closer than they were in the rural area where I grew up. People dressed differently and spoke without the southern dialect I was accustomed to hearing. I became conscious of the words I used. For example, instead of saying "carry" I said "tote." I soon removed that word from my vocabulary.

I had one other distinguishing characteristic besides my Southern accent, a gold tooth right in the front of my mouth. I had to get that gold tooth removed. Something that once gave me so much pride had now become a clear indicator of my rural roots. If I was going to have a new start, I needed a new image. I made an appointment with a dentist and had the crown removed. I felt like I had begun to find my way in my new life and started to look the part—not looking like the country girl that I was, but more like the northern city girl I wanted to become.

I felt like I was going to be all right in Michigan. I was learning my way around Detroit and realizing how much fun there was to be had in the big city.

Detroit offered lots of interesting opportunities for entertainment. There were night clubs all over town, and as time went on, I was introduced to many of them. We would often go to a

club call Watts Mozambique. Watts was a typical night club on most nights, and a male dancer club on the other nights. I started hanging out with Jean, a girl from Anniston Alabama, who was already familiar with the good clubs.

"Good" clubs I later learned were the ones where men would buy drinks for pretty women. One of those we attended on a regular basis was a place called the Boogie Down Club. It was small and offered different types of events, like fashion shows. We would go to the Boogie Down club to drink and dance. There was another club called Chuck's Millionaire Club and was considered the place where the "High Rollers" hung out.

Finally, there was the Detroit West Club which was known for a great dance floor and nice-looking men. My friend Carla would leave work and go there to save us seats. That was too early for me, but I'd arrive about 8:00 and meet her there. I eventually stopped going to the Detroit West Club as it had lost its appeal. As a recovering alcoholic, I did not enjoy drunk sweaty men hanging on me, or falling asleep at my table. I realized that as just not fun anymore.

Pregnant

Shortly after moving to Michigan I had some problems with my cycle being very irregular, which was not typical for a 21-year-old young woman. I went to the doctor when I started passing what appeared to be skin and tissue. The doctor said it appeared that I had experienced a miscarriage, and gave me a DNC procedure. I was shocked to find out that this is what had occurred.

I was also happy in some respects, because I thought I could actually get pregnant. Unfortunately, I never had any pregnancies after that. I am not even sure who that babies' father would have been, since I did not have a boyfriend at the time. I had only had a couple of one-night stands. It was like having a million dollars in my hands, and suddenly having it taken away.

Factory Life

My cousin's husband Tony, who had worked for Chrysler for a number of years, got me an interview for a job. Shortly after, I started working in the factory. The work was hard, but there was a smorgasbord of men to choose from. One day began like most in the factory, hot and miserable. I made my way to my spot in the assembly line and a guy walked over to where I was working.

"Hello," he said. "My name is Aaron. You're Tony's cousin, right?"

"Yes, I am Tony's cousin," I said, pleased to respond.

"Well, I just came to see if you needed anything." Aaron, said.

I was thinking anything like what.

"I have some cognac," he said.

"What's cognac?" I asked

"What? You've never had cognac."

I shook my head.

"I will be right back," he said and left. He couldn't have been gone more than a couple minutes then returned. "Here. Try this." He passed me a cup with coffee in it, and I tasted it.

"This is good!" I said, pleasantly surprised by the flavor. "Thanks."

That turned into a short-lived relationship, because I later learned he was already involved with a co-worker's sister.

After discovering this information, I also learned I had crabs. I had no idea what they were. I discovered them while in the bathroom, after scratching myself raw. I had Tony take me to the doctor, and he told me what I had. He gave me a prescription shampoo to treat the condition. Tony told Brenda, and she freaked out.

She said, "I thought only nasty girls got crabs!"

That made me feel even worse. I said, "I thought the same thing! Only nasty girls had them."

Tony came to my rescue. He told Brenda she was being too hard on me. Tony was my hero. He passed away a few years ago, shortly after being diagnosed with throat cancer. I will forever remember you Tony, rest in peace.

Factory life presented a whole new world. I heard terms such as "Factory Wife" and "Factory Husband." There were many other aspects of factory life that were head-turning. You could determine the culture in the factory by the department in which you worked. For example, the engine department was the alternative lifestyle area. My experience in the factory could fill another book. So, for now I will say that I experienced things in the factory that I have not experienced again.

No Self Worth

Burdened with a load of insane, unfounded, and unwarranted information, I had little to no self-worth. Knowing what I knew about myself and that I could not become pregnant, my mission in life shifted; I just wanted to have as much fun as I could. I had concluded that I had become damaged goods, and no decent man would want me for his wife. That wasn't what my heart desired, but in my mind having anything was better than nothing.

My next conquest in the factory was a young guy named Andre. He was friendly, and we went to lunch at the local watering hole to drink our lunch occasionally. There was no discussing or requesting a date or any of the usual dating rituals. We just became a couple, but this wasn't going to last long because neither of us had any idea about what a healthy relationship even looked like.

Andre was a young alcoholic and had an older sister who was a heroin addict. At that time, I didn't know what heroine was, or what it did for that matter.

Somehow, I always managed to attract men who were in worse shape than I was. Andre had only had one girlfriend according to one of his older friends. I was looking for a place to live at the time, and Andre introduced me to Linda. She lived in a two-family flat, and the upstairs was vacant. She had an unusual relationship with Andre and his friends, who were quite a bit younger than she was.

She did not hesitate to let me know she really liked Andre's previous girlfriend. Once again, I found myself competing for the man I had chosen. Andre was out messing around and I knew it, but I couldn't prove it. That is until I contracted vaginal warts, and that was all the proof I needed. Thanks for sharing your STD, Andre. This episode was just one more demeaning event that left me feeling worthless and alone. Andre continued to lie about his cheating, but I was done and broke it off with him.

I Choose You To Make Me Happy

As time went on, I found myself involved with a married man named Larry who worked in the same factory where I worked. He told me he was separated from his wife. We hung out and had some good times, because he was a very fun-loving person. I enjoyed that, as I had not had much fun in my life. Through this relationship I was introduced to chocolate mescaline, which was a high-powered form psychedelic. I can still remember how it made me feel.

A girl named Berenice worked on my line, and she noticed I was acting odd. I can remember saying, "Larry, you are so funny, and look at Charlotte. She looks like a cartoon."

"Why'd you say that?" he asked.

"Look at her hair!" I was laughing uncontrollably, and I had no idea it was the speed that had this effect on me. Mind you, I was working on the line in the factory and handling raw glass windshields.

Once again, my perfect relationship only lasted for a little while, as I noticed Larry leaving my house in the middle of the night. I soon realized he was going home to his wife and child. He made the excuse that he needed to be there to take care of his child. I had a hard time detaching myself from him and made a decision that I would do everything I could to destroy the marriage.

I continued in this relationship and even went as far as to try and get pregnant while involved with him. During this very unhealthy relationship, I went to a fertility specialist and discovered I had blockages in both fallopian tubes. There was no conclusive information about how this happened. However, I wanted to become pregnant so desperately I went forward with the surgery.

Not only did I not have a husband, I didn't even have a fulltime boyfriend. I didn't understand or consider that I needed to be either married, or at least in a committed relationship with someone who was going to be in my life consistently. I had only one goal in mind, and that was to have a baby. When that did not happen during this relationship, I gave up on the idea of becoming pregnant.

I had an encounter with Larry's wife after he had gone back home permanently. She followed me in her car as I drove and pulled up next to me one day as I was headed to work.

"Are you Sandra?" she asked.

"Who wants to know?" I shot back.

"My name is Evie," she said with an attitude, as we idled in the middle of the street talking.

I noticed she was very attractive woman and dressed quite nicely. I could also see inside her car and saw she had an open bottle liquor and a cup in her hand. I knew then who she was.

"So, you know who I am, right?" she asked.

"Yes, I know who you are."

"What is going on with you and my husband?" she wanted to know.

"We're just friends and co-workers."

She did not believe me and continued to question me about my involvement with him.

"You should ask your husband what is going on with us," I said and drove off.

I Love You

Once again, my low self-esteem, or more accurately, my non-existent self-esteem had me spiraling down the wrong road. When the factory job came to an end, and people were being laid off indefinitely, I found employment at a local department store chain in the music section. While working there I met a young man named Ronald Young, known to everyone as Ron, who was nice and friendly. That spoke volumes to me—a young woman who did not value herself. Ron came to my department often just to say hello.

I thought that I would invite him to my house, but I had no idea what I was getting myself into. I ran into him in another department in the store and said, "Hi Ron. What are you doing later?"

"I don't have anything planned."

"I was wondering if you'd like to come to my house for dinner."

"Sure," he said. "I would like that."

"Do you have a ride?" I asked.

"No, I don't have a car, but I can get someone to drop me off."

"Okay then, I'll see you later." That should have been a red flag, but I didn't let it deter me from pursuing him. Loneliness coupled with low self-esteem can make a person ignore the flashing red lights when it comes to making bad choices in life.

Ron came to my house, and I was taken in by his boyish charm. We ate dinner and made small talk. After dinner, I brought out some Cognac, and we had a few drinks. He left, and said we would see each other at work the next day. This went on for a while, and one day I said to him after seeing him for about a year, that I wanted to get married, and he agreed. It did not go over well with his mother and grandmother.

They wanted their baby boy to have a wedding and marry a girl named Lisa. Of course, Ron could not have paid for the gas money to get to the church for a wedding let alone pay for the whole thing. If they could have chosen someone for him to marry, it would have been Lisa, because she lived in the neighborhood where he grew up, and she had two babies that were supposed to be his. She was cute, and I could see how having babies made her the winner in my new competition for love. Ron sneaked around with Lisa and any other woman he could find to sleep with. He was a real charmer, because he had a boyish look and a great gift for gab.

I guess one could say, I could really pick the losers. All of the men that I somehow managed to involve myself with at that time were really outgoing. I supposed this characteristic is what attracted me to them, since I was essentially an introvert. I never considered that they were broke, unemployed, and didn't have a "pot to piss in or a window to throw it out of" as my mom would say. I thought that if I provided the money and the transportation, they would be committed to me and love me unconditionally. I was always wrong, and it seemed that the more I provided, the more they cheated and caused me pain.

I was often surprised by some of the women my men involved themselves with. They were rarely cute or smart, and some of them were far from being attractive in comparison to me. I knew Ron was cheating, but he would lie each time I approached him about it. One of his women followed me to my job, and called me.

She got right to the point. "My name is Roxie. Me and Ron

are involved, and I am pregnant."

My heart sank to the floor, but I was quick on the comeback. I said, "Then you should be calling him, don't you think?"

She went on to give me explicit details about their sex life. I shot back by saying I taught him everything he knew.

I was dying inside as I got off the phone with tears running down my face. Back then, beepers were in, and the cell phone had not been created yet. I beeped Ron, and he called me back. I told him his girlfriend Roxie had followed me to my job and called to let me know she was pregnant. Of course, he denied everything.

Later that day I heard that he beat her up badly, and that her brothers were looking for him.

There were many other similar incidences. Once, while armed with my gun, I went to confront one of the girls he was messing around with. There were others, and after arguing with them and feeling like crap, I stopped confronting them or trying to find out who the new chick on the side was. I gave up on trying to get him to care.

Lying About Having Babies

Over the years I had been privy to the types of offhanded negative things people would say about men only wanting women who could have babies. This led me to believe men do not want women who *can't* have children. Television and movies only confirmed my beliefs. In movies, I would often see men leaving their unfertile women and wives, to find younger, more beautiful, fertile women who could have children. I had this thought playing in my head like a bad song when I would meet men. Therefore, I had an expectation that men would not like me because I had not had any children. I knew for a fact that when they found out I was infertile; they would run in the other direction.

I met a man named Marsh who lived near me. He was the owner of a local gas station, which gave him status in the neighborhood. I liked him, and right away we started seeing each other, but that was short-lived because he had many women vying for his attention.

Somewhere during our brief fling, he asked me if I had children, and I told him that I did. I had to come up with something, and so I concocted a lie about actually having a baby who lived with my mother in Alabama. I went as far as to get a picture of my cousin's baby, Tamiko, a beautiful little girl, and showed it off to unsuspecting men.

My relationship with Marsh soon ended, because I became tired of telling that lie after a while. I saw myself as an empty shell of a woman, and I needed something to make me feel better about myself. I could not see how beautiful I was, or how much I had to offer because only one thing in my mind determined a woman's worth, and that was giving birth to a child. I wanted that more than anything, and nothing I could do was going to make it happen. Remember, mindsets where I came from proclaimed that women who couldn't have babies were mostly useless.

According to the great poet, Alfred Lord Tennyson, "'Tis better to have loved and lost than never to have loved at all." In my case, I believe that's true. For all the relationships I've had, good and bad, I've come away from them much wiser. More importantly, I've come away a better person.

Introduction to Cocaine

As time went on, I tried everything to make Ron be the person I wanted him to be. I wanted him to have a loving soft side and also have the "bad boy" side as well. However, he only knew the bad boy side, because he had not had a positive role model in his life, ever. His father was a known pimp in his time, and his stepfather was a drug dealer and addict. The relationship with Ron was abusive on many levels, and I was sinking deeper and deeper into depression.

In this marriage, I soon discovered that I had no allies in his mother or grandmother. Betty and Granny, Ron's mother and grandmother, made it painfully clear they had no interest in being kind to me or showing me love in any way. They went above and beyond the call of duty to let it be known they not only loved Ron's children that he had with Lisa, but they also loved her dearly.

I often think that they carried on the way they did about the children intentionally to hurt me. If hurting me was what they were trying to do, it worked more than they would ever know. They would often bring the children around, and it was torture.

One of the things I learned is that people can be cruel when they know your weakness. It was no secret I wanted a baby, and they used that to make the hurt more intense. I went on with life, but on the inside I was miserable. The cheating continued, and I was alone to deal with all of my thoughts and feelings, and I just wanted an escape route. I felt that life was useless, and no man wanted me.

This relationship propelled me to find a way to medicate all the disappointment and pain inflicted not only in this relationship but throughout my life. That is when I was introduced to cocaine. At first, it was just a little snorting from time to time. I didn't even know what to do or what to expect. Along the way, I soon became a pro at it, because I wanted to feel anything but the feelings life had dealt me. Like all the things that I attempted in my life, I sought perfection in this newfound option as well.

Free Basing

One night while hanging out with my girlfriend, Jean, one of her friends came by, and they started smoking something in a little glass pipe. I wanted to try it, because it looked like fun, and of course I had already snorted cocaine, though I wasn't hooked on it.

"Jean, I want to try that," I said. On that particular night I had one hit and didn't really notice or feel anything. However, in typical Sandra Pugh fashion I just had to get it right. So, I reached out to the guy at Jeans house, whose name I forget.

He said, "Come sit by me. Try it."

I slid next to him on the sofa.

"What's your name?" he asked.

"Sandra."

"You're really cute, girl. You got a boy-friend?"

"No," I said, "I don't have a boyfriend. Actually, I'm married."

He placed a small pebble-like object in the glass pipe and lit it with a cigarette lighter. Then he let me have a pull, or what he called a "hit." That meant to place the pipe between your lips, pull hard, and inhale deeply. I didn't even know what I was hoping would happen. After a few experiences free basing with Jean and her friends, I wanted to try it again.

Getting The Right Paraphernalia

I told another friend, named Cassandra, about this free basing thing, and she said that she did it also. Cassandra said she would show me how to freebase "the right way." She picked me up, and we went to her house in Southfield. She had a really nice apartment in a good neighborhood. I was impressed with how she was living since I was still in the "hood." Sandra had beautiful modern furniture and expensive clothes, and she was driving a new car.

We went into her basement, and it was furnished with new

furniture as also. Sandra, you have a really lovely place here. Yea it's alright for now, I really want to buy a house. Sandra had a boyfriend named Curtis—a "Sugar Daddy" because he was much older. "Curtis bought all of this furniture for me and my son," Cassandra said.

Sandra had a big glass pipe. When she put the cocaine in it and lit it, the bowl filled up with smoke. Jean's friend's pipe never filled up like that. Cassandra explained, "It's because they didn't know what they were doing. When you pull it, let your lungs fill up."

I put the stem to my lips and pulled lightly on the pipe; the rest is history. The feeling that came from the hit of rock cocaine was like nothing I had ever experienced. I wanted to buy a pipe like the one she had. Cassandra told me where I could get a pipe like hers. She drove me to my house where my experienced, drug-using husband was waiting so we could continue getting high. Just like everything else I had done in my life, I wanted to get it right.

My Mama Died, And Something Died In Me

Somewhere in the middle of all of the insanity, I received a phone call from my cousin Mae Frances, who let me know Mama was in the hospital. I always loved Mae Frances, and I will be forever grateful that she cared enough about me to let me know Mama was sick. We had some problems, but I believe that the love between us never died. I was at one of the lowest points in my life and had gone to Cincinnati, Ohio, to spend time with Jean O, which was what we called her. Jean O is my biological sister, who had been raised by another woman named Naomi.

When I arrived at her house, I hoped I could have a fresh start. I soon discovered that Jean O was getting high with her boyfriend, Stanley, on a regular basis, and on a much grander scale than I had ever experienced. She talked about her experience with drugs, and I could tell this was not going to be a good place to recover or start a new life.

I wasn't sure what I was going to do or where I was going. So, when I received the call from my cousin, I just knew I had to get home to see about my mama. Jean had an older friend who was like her sugar daddy, and she got him to pay for our airline tickets to Alabama. This would be her first trip back to Alabama in years, and I could tell she wanted to see her grandmother and her father, who lived in Anniston. We arrived and immediately went to the hospital to see Mama. She was overjoyed to see both of us, but unfortunately, Jean could not stay for long as she had to get back to her children.

The Day My Mama Died

It was November 9, 1986 around 12:00 a.m., and I had just crawled into bed when the phone rang. It was the charge nurse at the hospital where my mother was a patient. She explained that my mother had taken a turn for the worst, and they needed to know if I wanted them to place her on the respirator. In just a matter of seconds I experienced a range of emotions, as fear gripped me and almost paralyzed my entire being. My heart raced, and my stomach instantly knotted. I felt sad, and I felt hot and cold at the same time.

I knew my mother did not want to be on a respirator, because she had talked about sitting with her friend, Ms. Carpenter, while she was sick and hooked to a respirator. She had described in detail the sounds the machine made as it kept her friend alive, but in a vegetative state. She told me in no uncertain terms that she did not want to be placed on "one of those machines."

I knew if I said "yes" I would not be honoring my mother's wishes, but if I said no, her death would be inevitable and would most certainly come quickly. I wanted to not have to make that decision. I climbed out of bed on shaky legs and stood upright so I could catch my breath.

Just a few seconds passed, but it felt like an eternity, and I could hear the nurse breathing on the other end, waiting for my response. I was finally able to speak, and I could hear myself saying, "No, I do not want her placed on the respirator."

The nurse said I should probably get there as soon as I could. I managed to get myself ready to go somehow. There was much more mental preparation than physical. I took a quick shower while the tears flowed down my face.

I had been putting on quiet a performance for a few months, because my mother had told me emphatically over the years that she did not want to know if she was dying. So, when she had been hospitalized for the first time ever about three months earlier, and the terminal cancer diagnosis was confirmed to me by her physician, I made it clear that she was not to be told.

I spent my days with her from August to November knowing this horrible truth, and not letting on that anything seriously was wrong. When she went back in the hospital for dehydration, I was able to cry without interruption, and I thought the tears would never end. When the tears finally stopped, I felt as though my body was empty. It was somewhat of a catharsis, which allowed me to then spend time with my mother without showing any sadness.

Moreover, just a few days before her death, while visiting her in the hospital, she asked me if she was dying. Of course, I lied and said no, that she just needed to make sure she ate her food and she would be better soon. I could not stop the tears this time; they flowed down my face and onto my shirt until it was soaked.

Later that morning, after getting the call from the hospital, I stood in my mother's hospital room more afraid than I had ever been, listening to the sounds and taking in the smells that I will never forget. I watched my mother pass away as I held her hand. I can still hear her crying out "I'm dying," as she took her last breaths. I felt a sadness deep in my soul that I had never experienced before. The kind of sadness and heartbreak that took my breath away. My life was forever changed on that day, because I knew the love of my mother could never be replaced.

I didn't see Jean again until after mama died, when she came for the funeral. The funeral was drama-filled to say the least. I had to send for Fannie Mae, because she had no money to buy her own bus ticket. On the day of the funeral, Fannie Mae was drinking beer. I had to ask her to put it up before the funeral directors came to take us to the church. It was clear Jean was upset that I was getting on Fannie about her drinking. She wanted us to be one big happy family, and that clearly was not happening.

Jean left shortly after the funeral, but Fannie stayed on for a little while, just long enough to give me a hard time about whether or not mama had any money. She said she wanted to see Mama's bank books. I told her everything was in my name, and there was no money. Fannie had been talking to our cousin who told her that mama did have money, and she should go to the bank and get it before I spent it all.

None of this went well, and when I told her there was a will and that we would go to the lawyer and let him read it on Monday, she appeared to be all right with how it would be handled. Unfortunately, when alcohol is a factor, things can go downhill really quickly. And that is what happened. After the funeral she went to Mae France's house and got drunk.

She came in and said she wanted to read the will, and I gave it to her. When she read the part where it stated that Mama willed me everything and left her one dollar, she went off. She said, "This goddamn will ain't real, and I know that my mama had money!" One thing led to another, and I told her to get out. She called our cousin to come and get her. She came back later to get her things, and I told her she could take any of Mama's clothes that she wanted. She took a few things and left. Years passed before I saw her, or Jean, or any of her other children again.

The Hardest Blow

As Ron sank deeper into crack cocaine addiction, he would be gone for days and at other times would stay at his mama's house. Betty would lie and say she had not heard from him when I would call to see if he was there. On the other hand, I was getting better, and I started attending Narcotics Anonymous Meetings. I managed to put together about 10 months of clean time and was feeling pretty good about myself for the first time in my life.

I would hear from Ron every now and then, but I was pretty sure he was getting high all the time and staying at his mama's house. The hardest blow came when I discovered he was having an affair with a girl named Sonja. I went to where he worked and confronted them. He said he wanted to be with her. I somehow got her phone number and called, hoping to reason with her. Nothing worked.

I was shocked when I received a phone call from her mother threating me because I was calling her daughter's workplace. She said, "I already been to prison, and I will kill anybody that messes with my daughter." I was shocked and asked if she was really calling me to tell me she was all right with her daughter being involved with my husband.

I later found out Sonja was pregnant. I was devastated, and the pain never went away. I had to endure hearing about Ron and Sonja and their baby from people who knew us both. I didn't have many people in my life, and the few I did have found it necessary to align themselves with Ron. I wanted someone to have some loyalty for me, but that didn't happen. Not at first anyway, but ultimately my temporary sponsor, Larry, became a great friend and ally.

On the day I received this devastating information, I was so hurt that I called my old "Sugar Daddy" and asked him to bring me something to drink. He did, and I drank until I was drunk. I had heard that once you have achieved some level of recovery, getting high would not be as great as it once was. I felt that instantly when I relapsed, and I felt really disappointed in myself. I was a failure. You see something was changing inside of me, and I hadn't even noticed it. Being involved with a married man just didn't feel right anymore. I could not be with him, and I just wanted to get away from him.

I called my friend, Leslie, and told her what happened. She came over immediately and took me to a meeting. I had only been drinking that one day, and because of Leslie's caring heart, I was able to get back on track with my recovery. And even though I was hurting badly, I was able to get back to making Narcotics Anonymous Meetings and re-start the process to recovery.

Pain Was My Motivator

Pain can sometimes be a motivator to change your life and start on a path to healing. I contacted a lawyer and filed for my divorce. That was the last time I got high, and it has now been over 30 years since my last drink or drug.

After being in recovery for a short period of time, I started seeing a therapist, and she was amazing. Joyce Martel was an older White woman, and in the beginning I wasn't sure if I would be all right with having her as my therapist, but I soon discovered she was a wonderful person. She had a unique gift for making you feel good about yourself. She would say, "Sweetheart you need to learn to love yourself." I will always remember Joyce, and how she used her skills for counseling to help me start my path to loving myself.

Recovery And Relapse

Getting high for me was recreational at first, and in the beginning I mostly did it when I had extra money. Looking back, I really believe it made me feel like I was the "cool girl." I learned how to medicate my feelings with alcohol and drugs. Having a husband who was severely addicted to drugs, I knew getting high occasionally would not last for long.

At some point I got tired of getting high, and I wanted Ron and I to go into recovery together. This idea did not work, because Ron had met someone he knew while he was in the treatment facility, and he was going out and getting high with him before coming back to the rehab facility at night. Since that behavior was not tolerated, he was kicked out of the program.

I, on the other hand finished my program, but coming home to a husband who continued to get high was not helpful at all. It t wasn't long before I joined right in.

I had heard and seen some things during Narcotics Anonymous (NA) meetings that had me thinking my short stint with drugs was not that bad at all. I eventually realized that drugs were a symptom of my addiction. In Narcotics anonymous I was told that addiction was all about ones behavior and getting high resulted from the behavior, which in turn could be seen as a symptom.

I was still a loner, and I wasn't trying to make friends with any of the other women in the program. I guess my antennas went up when I heard some of their horror stories during the meetings. One woman shared her experience about being seduced by another female in the program who was outwardly gay. That had me running in the other direction when it came to being involved with women.

Of course, I had some internal messages of my own about women, and I wasn't trying to repeat any of those things that I had experienced. As time went on, I was able to get close with one or two females, but I kept them at arms-length. Or maybe they kept *me* at arms-length. Remember, we were all on our own paths to recovery.

I Knew God

I had been introduced to God and religion at an early age, and I knew that God was all about love. I started to pray for some relief from all the pain and hurt and disappointment that I experienced throughout my life. I got back in church and renewed my relationship with God. Life was getting better, and I was seeing myself in a new light. I continued to see my therapist Joyce, an amazing woman who taught me about loving myself. She also showed me how to love my inner child which was something I had never thought about.

For the next seven years or so, I was alone with just me and my thoughts. I attended a lot of NA meetings and NA dances, and this added some fun to my life. I tried to get into relationships, but it just was not working for me. I decided to register for some classes at Henry Ford Community College. I was a first-generation college student, and I had no idea what went on in higher education. However, these things allowed me to stay busy and keep my mind off my loneliness.

I had decided that once I finished college I would move back to Alabama. Fortunately, God had another plan and after meeting the love of my life, I stayed on in Michigan.

God Gave Me A Baby

I thought that giving birth to a baby was the only way a woman could have a child to love, but God showed me a different way. I was feeling good about everything God was doing in my life, and I wanted to help someone else. While sitting at my desk at work one day, I heard an announcement on the radio for the "Adopt a Child for Christmas" program. I called the number they provided and was told someone would contact me with the name of a child and all of that child's information. When the call came, I learned the child's name, Ishamia, her clothing size, and the date of the event which would be held at Cobo Hall in downtown Detroit.

I took the little money I had and bought a few items of clothing and a stuffed animal for the little three-year-old I was going to meet to deliver the things I purchased. On that day in late December, I showed up at the Adopt a Child for Christmas banquet and was surprised to see all the people there with their children, and the individuals who were providing gifts for them. When the event was over, I gave Ishamia's young mom, Arnell, and her mother, Debra Turner, my telephone number. I never really expected to hear from them again.

A few months later, on Mother's Day, I received a call from Arnell and Ishamia. On the phone was a tiny little voice. "Hi, Sandra. It's Arnell and Ishamia, and we wanted to wish you a Happy Mother's Day." I was so excited to hear from them, and I could not stop the tears from raining down my face. No one had ever recognized me on this special day, and I was overjoyed.

I went to visit them and realized they really needed help.

71

Well, I thought, I needed love. I thought I could help them, and they could give me some of the love I'd missed my entire life. Ishamia and Arnell became my babies and remain an amazing part of my life. They continue to share their love with me. I now have the ability to say without lying, that I have babies.

Finding Love in a Stinky Supermarket

"Love recognizes no barriers. It jumps hurdles, leaps fences, penetrates walls to arrive at its destination full of hope." —Maya Angelou

One Christmas Eve while dragging Ishamia along, I went looking for pie crust. She and her mother were visiting with me, and I was cooking dinner for Christmas Day and needed pie crust. After going to Farmer Jacks, one of the large supermarket chains in our neighborhood, and not finding a single pie crust, I decided to go to one of the smaller stores in the neighborhood.

When Ishamia and I were getting out of my car, I noticed an Alcoholics Anonymous sticker on the bumper of a car that had just pulled up. I said to the driver, "I like the sticker on your car." When we got inside the store the passenger in the car approached Ishamia and me and stared to tell me all about himself.

He said, "My name is David, and I am a born-again Christian. I'm a nice man, and if you want to go to dinner sometime, here is my number." I was looking a total mess. I had on a hat to cover my undone hair, no makeup, my clothes were covered in drippings from cooking, and I was dragging a three-year-old along who wasn't in much better shape. I was also unsure if I wanted to date anyone, especially since my history with dating had been a disaster.

I took the phone number and tucked it in my pocket. I didn't think much about it, but Ishamia must have been, because when we got back to the house, she told her mother, "Sandra met a man at the supermarket and him was cute."

I said, "*You* thought he was cute."

She replied with a simple, "Un huh."

Well, "out of the mouths of babes" came what I think of as a prophetic word, and it prompted me to give David a call. At that time cell phones were just becoming popular, and we were calling from home phones and leaving messages on message machines.

God's Man For Me

David called me back and we planned to go out. I wasn't sure what to think of this man. He was fun-loving and really enjoyed food. We went out on a few dates to eat and talk. He took me to the East side of Detroit, down on the river, to see all of the Christmas decorations, and I dozed off in the car. He could have taken offense at that, but he didn't. I guess he understood I was just tired. At some point we laughed about me going to sleep during our first date. I explained that I loved to sleep when riding in a car.

After dating for about a year, we started talking more seriously about marriage. I was scared to think I could be getting married a third time. I prayed about it and talked about it a lot with my friend Darling, affectionately known as "Darlene." One Saturday night, David and I had plans to go out to a local comedy club called Bea's Comedy Kitchen. At some point during the evening, he pulled out a ring and asked me to marry him, and I said yes. When the waitress came to our table, I told her that he just proposed and I had accepted. Well, of course she told the comedian, and he announced it to the whole audience. I was worried he might try to make jokes about it, but he was nice and didn't say anything silly.

We did not have a wedding, for a number of reasons. For one thing, David had not been divorced that long. He was married for only about 4 months, and had only been divorced for a year or so. Also, because I was still concerned what people might think about me, or him. I don't know why; I suppose my low self-esteem drove that line of thought. Looking back, I can see how we probably should have given him a little more time to heal from the disappointing and sudden end to his short second marriage.

David explained that he and wife number two only dated for a short period before they married. Soon afterward, she decided she had made a mistake, and according to David she really loved someone else more. He also talked about how deeply that hurt him.

Immediately, I was jealous of the woman he had divorced. I'd never met the woman, but I felt I was competing with her. I suppose it was because he had loved her so deeply. He said he went into a deep depression when she told him she was divorcing him because she had made a mistake and chose the wrong man. David explained that his ex-wife had been dating him and another man at the same time. She divorced David and married the other man.

David talked about her with deep affection. She was going to have her tubes untied and have a baby with him, and I knew that was what he wanted badly. She was bi-racial like his mother, and his family loved her. She was everything he thought he wanted, and when she left him, he was hurt deeply.

I did not want to be the rebound girl, but he convinced me he was over her and wanted to move on. He often said he wanted his own family. I had to tell him I was pretty sure that I could not have any babies. I wanted to make sure he understood that and would be all right with knowing it. He assured me he was okay with it. I felt we had a lot in common, and that we could have a happy life together.

Even though I was scared to death, I made a decision to marry him.

We were married in my church by Pastor Adams. My best friend Larry gave me away.

David later joined my church. We spent our honeymoon in Puerto Vallarta, Mexico. The days

were sunny and bright, and we enjoyed every minute together. We laid in the sun at the pool and walked along the beautiful sandy beach. We visited some of the outdoor shops that were near our hotel. Everyone was very friendly, and even though neither one of us spoke a word

of Spanish, we were able to communicate well. We went on tours into the jungle areas and never felt any fear or harm. One of my fondest memories was the tour we took up into the mountains. Along the shore there were some of the most beautiful houses I have ever seen. The houses were positioned high above the blue, coastal waters.

Our tour stopped, and everyone got out to view the beautiful homes and seashore. The natives in the area stood along the route and displayed large iguanas. We took pictures standing near a man holding a very large one. He offered to let us hold the iguana, but I immediately refused the offer. I think David considered it, but then refused the offer as well.

We also viewed a bull fight. I had no idea what a bull fight entailed, and so we made our way to the arena. I should have known something was wrong when the horses were brought into the arena wearing blind folds. Things soon went downhill from that point. The man on the horse began stabbing the bull with a long spear he was carrying, and the crowd roared. At some point, as the fight became gorier and bloodier, I covered my eyes.

People were laughing and appeared to be enjoying the event,

but I told David I could not take anymore, and we left. I was later informed that they killed three bulls during the event. It was also mentioned that the meat was donated to local food banks. I guess that was supposed to make me feel better, but it did not. I knew I would never go to another bull fight.

I had the most memorable time of my life. In my wildest dreams, I never thought I would be able to travel to a place like the one where we spent the first week of our married life together. I will never forget how excited my husband was about everything we did. The food was different, but I enjoyed many of the exotic Mexican dishes. David ate everything in sight, and smiled from ear to ear. It felt as if time stood still.

At some point, I remember fear setting in. I wondered when my happiness would give way to something sad, and unhappiness would take over. My life had been a series of disappointments and unhappiness, and I was afraid we could not overcome all of the misery we had both experienced. At the same time, however, I was determined to not let all those past disappointments destroy the possibilities for love that lay ahead.

We left Mexico and headed to the airport to come back to the United States and a return to reality. I was ready for us to get on with our lives together, and learn how to enjoy this beautiful man God had given me.

The first five years were hard because as much as we wanted love, and wanted to love each other, we were not doing well. I still had trust issues and was not convinced he would remain faithful and not beat on me. Though he'd given me no reason to doubt him, I still expected him to do something that would break my heart, but he never has. He has been loyal and fully committed to our marriage. He has never cheated on me or abused me in any way. He has tried to give me everything I ever asked for, and I know his love is pure and genuine.

I love the soft side of the man that he is, because he can feel the pain of other people and empathize with them. He has the biggest heart and loves to help those who are less fortunate. Actually, he is the total opposite of all the other men I have ever been involved with. He is my knight in shining armor as I wrote many years ago, in the poem below simply titled David:

DAVID

Bright as the new sun
That shouts to the darkness be gone!
Like knights of old
Chivalry reborn
Gentle as petals on a rose

Gallant as knights of old

Bright is the armor that

Covers your soul

My knight in shining armor

Like the knights of old

In-Laws Or Outlaws

When I first met David's family, he left me alone to fend for myself. He was so scared of them he could not even defend himself. I discovered he had been considered—and treated—as the "Black Sheep" of his family. No one ever actually said it, but I based my conclusions on the way his brothers treated him; it was apparent how they felt about him.

I can remember once when David's oldest brother came into town and didn't bother to call him to let him know he was there. David found out from his other brother, Raymond, that George was in town. He was clearly hurt, and I could feel his pain. I called George's wife, Ruth, and told her what I thought about how George had treated my husband. I already knew they didn't care for me, and so I just took to defending the man I love. Of course, he did not want me to say anything to them, because he wanted them to like him. I told him he should defend himself and grow some balls.

David is not a confrontational person, and so confronting them never happened. I worried at one point he might start drinking again, just so he would be accepted by them. Fortunately, he remained sober, and as the years have gone by his people have finally accepted the fact that he is not going to drink alcohol.

Not one of David's four sisters showed any interest in getting to know me. I thought for sure since there were four of them, I would connect with one, but I was dead wrong.

The Depression War

"When life brings you down and makes you sad,
let angels lift you high and make you glad." –Sandra Pugh

Life experiences leave behind residue, and sometimes it lasts a lifetime. That residue can take on many forms. Sometimes it is unresolved anger, mistrust, and at other times it is the inability to forgive. Residue can also come in the form of depression and anxiety. I have fought each one of these residual demons throughout my life. In my fight I have used every bit of ammunition made available. I even tried medication once, but I did not like the way it made me feel.

I have also observed the severe side effects of certain medications on some of my closest friends. Leslie was an amazing person; she was already in recovery when I showed up, and she was so sweet. We became good friends, and when I relapsed after ten months of being clean, Leslie came to my rescue. She had been a few years clean, and she was able to help me understand the importance of recovery. You might ask what could possibly happen that would cause a person to relapse after being clean for seven years. Leslie was fired from her job, and she became severely depressed. She listened to some advice that led her to a doctor who did not give thought to the medication he prescribed for her.

After taking some very strong medication for over a year, Leslie wanted to try and stop taking it, but the withdrawal symptoms were too hard for her to handle on her own. So, she checked herself into a facility to try and withdraw. Unfortunately, the attempt was unsuccessful, and she started to seek street drugs to help her cope. It wasn't long before her addiction took control of her life again.

I tried on numerous occasions to reach Leslie but was unable to contact her. At some point I found Leslie's mother's phone number and called her. I had to make her remember who I was, and once she did, she told me that Leslie had died. She went on to explain that Leslie got back on heroine and was found dead in an abandoned building. I was shocked and devastated by what I heard and could not stop the tears from coursing down my face. I told Leslie's mother that I loved her daughter and had tried to get her to go to meetings with me, but she would not go. She always had an excuse. I also told her that I owed Leslie a debt of gratitude for helping me get back on track with my recovery. Leslie's death spoke volumes to me about the importance of staying clean and not using drugs or alcohol. Leslie saved my life, and I will be forever grateful for her love and concern. Rest in Gods arms, Leslie.

God Gave Me a Second Baby

I had a dream about a baby. In the dream the baby was right beside me, and I would be loving her, but then she would be far away from me. I thought how odd that I would have this dream, especially with my history of wanting to have a baby. Could it mean I was going to have a baby? Shortly after getting married, I met a young woman who sang in the choir at my church. Her name was Alicia, and she was pregnant. She asked me and David to be her baby's Godparents, and we agreed. Little did I know how much drama would come with that agreement. It soon became apparent this was not going to be good.

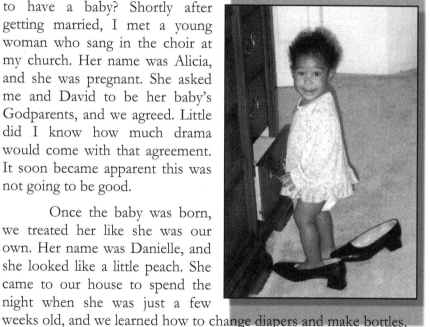

Once the baby was born, we treated her like she was our own. Her name was Danielle, and she looked like a little peach. She came to our house to spend the night when she was just a few weeks old, and we learned how to change diapers and make bottles.

We fell deeply in love with her, because neither of us had children. We wanted all the best for her. We thought about how we could make her life great. We bought her expensive clothes and toys and took them to her. At some point, I realized those clothes were not being cared for, and that did not make me happy.

Once when Danielle was visiting with us, I heard deep,

gurgling sounds in her lungs. I told David something was wrong and that she needed to go to the doctor. We were very concerned about her. When I told Alicia, she said nothing was wrong with her. It soon became apparent that none of her friends liked me. They thought I was getting too involved in her business, and that I should leave her alone.

I went to talk to Pastor Adams about all this, and I told him I did not want to be the godmother anymore, and I wanted him to tell me how I could get out of it. Unfortunately, he said Danielle needed me. He also stated that she was my ministry. Once, I saw it in that prospective, I was willing to try it again.

The drama did not stop. Not only were her young friends giving me problems, even her older friends like Loletha Smith, the church Choir Director, were encouraging her to treat us badly. Looking back, I don't think Loletha liked me because I was beautiful and had a husband who didn't cheat on me. I suspect the fact she had children of her own made her a child expert in Alicia's eyes. She also often held big drinking parties at her house, and several of the women from the church went there to spend time with her. That made her very popular.

At some point I just removed myself from Danielle's life, but as God would have it, we managed to find ourselves right back in it again. The catalyst for this came when Alicia took Danielle to the doctor who diagnosed the child with a heart condition that would require surgery. Alicia would never admit that my insistence was the reason she took Danielle to the doctor. Alicia actually told people she was the one who discovered the problem. Getting credit for Danielle receiving the help she needed is not important. I am just happy that God was able to use me in that situation.

Alicia was living in the worst conditions, a bug and rat-infested house. None of this seemed to bother Alicia or her friends. Of course, that is because they lived in similar conditions. When I visited her house the first time, I became concerned. I spoke with David about what I had discovered, and he wanted to take the baby out of that squalor. I agreed but reminded him we had no voice in the matter.

A few years later Danielle visited us. We went to a

playground, and I noticed she got tired quite easily. I knew I had to tell Alicia about what I had discovered, and once again she was not happy that I said something was wrong with her baby. By then I was the talk of the church. She told people I was trying to take her baby, and people looked at us like we were the enemy. None the less, when she did decide to take Danielle to the doctor it was determined she needed to have heart surgery again.

Trying to love another person's child cost me my reputation and the peace of mind I had come to know. I suppose some of the women once again were looking for a good reason to not like me, and this gave them the opportunity to show how they felt. Their most common refrain was, "She should have her own baby." I like to think this mostly came from those who were miserable, didn't have a man, and couldn't buy one with all the gold in the US Mint.

I hated Alicia for what she did, but most of all I was upset that she had allowed us to fall in love with the baby, and then decided we would not be part of her life. Not only were we not seen as a positive influence in her life, we certainly were not seen as family. Danielle would still come and visit from time to time, but it was apparent she had been drilled that we were just godparents and not family.

As time went on, I heard her speak of Loletha her husband Dexter and their children as family. I was hurt by all that was said and done, and I just wanted out of the situation. I prayed God would deliver me from needing to shop for Danielle or needing to have her in our home on a regular basis. I didn't want any part of it anymore, not because I didn't love her, but because I wanted the heartache to stop.

My husband did not feel quite as I felt because he wanted a relationship with this baby. He had fallen in love with the child as well. He tried to continue to communicate with her, but everyone knew how I felt about everything, and it just wasn't working. I have learned that people want you to operate on their terms at all times, and when you don't, you are excluded.

I discovered after months of no involvement with Danielle that Alicia claimed we were mistreating the girl. She sent Danielle over to where we were sitting in church, and we sent her back to her.

Alicia and her friends had done everything they could to discourage our involvement with Danielle, but when we did as they wanted and stopped having anything to do with her, she managed to make us seem like the bad guys again.

My husband and I did not let that deter us; we kept our distance. At times we would call or buy gifts, but we decided to stop as Danielle grew older and would not even call to check on us. She is a teen ager now and recently had to have open heart surgery for the third time.

We called her and sent a little gift to cheer her up, but we did not go to Michigan to see her. We understand our place in her life now, and we adhere to that. We finally let it sink in that we are not loved like the many people that are a part of her life. She doesn't see us as people who love her unconditionally, but rather as people who are distant and outside of the love circle.

Learning To Love Myself

Learning to love myself has been a real struggle, because I received so many negative reinforcements as a child and a young woman. Allowing God to heal all of the wounds of my past is an ongoing daily challenge, but it gets better every day. I know for a fact that God has angels watching over us, because I have seen my angel before. No, I am not crazy, and yes, I believe God has angels assigned to everyone.

When I lived in Michigan and experienced a really stressful period, I remember being asleep and waking up to seeing a shadow covering my bedroom window. I thought to myself, there is no tree in front of my home, so what could that possibly be? As my eyes adjusted, I could tell it was the shadow an angel hovering over my window. At that point, I realized angels are not small; they are very large beings. After seeing this wonderful thing, I became convinced God was looking out for me and that he still cared.

During my efforts to understand my self-loathing, I worked with an amazing counselor. When I was referred to Joyce, a White female, I wasn't sure how well that was going to work. I didn't know if she would have my best interests in mind. Remember, my southern roots and all of the blatant racism I had dealt with. Once I had a chance to get to know her however, I realized that she was very caring. I told her the reason I was so comfortable with her was because she had 11 children, and I thought only Black women had that many babies. She laughed at that, and we developed a wonderful professional relationship. We were able to do some tremendous healing work through those sessions.

I see myself as a worthy person today—at least most days I do—a person who deserves love and respect and the best God has to offer. The pain of never having been able to have my own baby is still there at times, but I know that this one piece of my womanhood does not define me totally. I understand today that I am so much more than just a vessel for giving birth. I am a person designed by God, and I am complete.

I still struggle with the idea of having someone to care for me in my old age, but like everything else I know God will provide when that time comes. I also believe and trust that some of the children I have loved will care enough to come care for me when I can no longer care for myself.

Sandra J. Pugh

God Gave Me Friends

"Lots of people want to ride with you in the limo, but what you want is someone who will take the bus with you when the limo breaks down." –Oprah Winfrey

Life for me was getting better. I could tell because I started to feel good about myself. For the first time in my life, I could enjoy being alone in my home or go to a movie by myself. The future had possibilities, and I wanted to consider them.

Getting out and having fun was a consideration, but I really didn't have any friends to go out with. There was a girl where I worked who mentioned that she went out to a night club not far from me. The place was called the "Detroit West Club" which was known for great music and drinks. My co-worker, Carla, would go after work and get a table; her friend Vivian and others would come later. I went too, from time to time and it was great fun.

As time went on, Carla and I became really close, and a friendship soon developed. Carla was great with her finances, and as a result loaned me money once in a while. I really appreciated her kindness, but I was afraid to get really close to anybody back then, especially women. Over time, as my self-esteem improved, I have been able to develop a great friendship with Carla, and I love her dearly.

When I went into recovery, I knew very few people there. Ron's aunt, Idelma known around the Narcotics Anonymous (NA) fellowship as Toni, was one of the people I knew. Idelma was dating a man named Larry, and he was a really nice person. Larry and Idelma broke up, but I would still see him around the fellowship at meetings. I would hear him sharing at meetings, and I got a chance to know him really well.

Larry started dating another person, and I got to know her really well also. In the beginning Terry was my sponsor, but after we had the big falling out, I did not have a sponsor. The NA program suggests that women have women sponsors and men have men sponsors. I was not about to ask any of those women to be my sponsor, so I asked Larry to be my temporary sponsor, and he agreed.

Larry was different from any of the men I had known in my life. He appeared to have morals and values, and I didn't think men even existed who were like that. I became a part of a family of recovering people, and I loved that idea. Larry also sponsored another woman named Gwen, which made me know that I had made a great choice for sponsorship. When I met my current husband David and decided to get married, I asked Larry to give me away, and he was more than happy to do it. Larry told David that he was happy to be in my life.

Looking back on my life before David, I can see why Larry was so happy about me getting married. During my then short time in recovery, I had gone through all of the drama leading up to my divorce with my ex-husband Ron, which was a horrible mess. Then I tried dating a few guys in the fellowship which all ended in disappointment. The final straw occurred when I dated Larry's sponsor, Dwight, who broke up with me over the phone while I was visiting friends in Alabama. I cried to Larry about all of these heartbreaks. He was my sounding board, and made no judgements.

I gained great respect for Larry through all of those love-gone-wrong relationships, because he never once tried to take advantage of me during this difficult time. Instead, he offered some of the best advice I had ever received in my life, which was to be good to myself. I consider Larry one of my best friends, and I will always love and respect him. Today I still respect his advice and love his candid way of reinforcing NA Program principles, making them applicable to every-day life occurrences.

My friend Pearlie lives in Alabama, in my old hometown; our friendship goes back for many years. Pearlie is a few years older than I am, and she is one of the sweetest people I know. When I was a teenager, Pearlie and her family moved into James Green's old house, which was right up the road from where I lived at the time. We all went to the same places like ball games, Cleaves, and Lint's to find our fun. I hung out with her sister Deb because she was more of the partying kind than Pearlie.

Over the years Pearlie purchased a small parcel of land close to where my mama lived, and they became really close after I moved to Michigan. Pearlie would take her anywhere she needed to go. She and her children all loved my mama. That meant so much to me, because Mama lived by herself and did not drive.

I started to communicate with Pearlie and grew closer; she was always nice to me. I was able to let down my guard and talk to her about everything—how I felt about the Green family and my other cousins. I could confide in Pearlie, and she would find a way to make things lighthearted. I always left our conversations feeling loved, something I had not felt in a long time.

After Mama died, and I would go home, I always went to Pearlie's house where I felt safe and comfortable. When David and I go to Alabama, we always spend time with Pearlie and James. I love her dearly and have the utmost respect for her. She is my sister from another mother, and I am forever grateful for all of the love she has shown me. When we go home now, we go to her house and love every minute of the time that we spend with them.

My friend Jan has come into my life in the last 10 years; she is an amazing and beautiful spirit. I met Jan at an NA meeting, and she was so friendly. She called us friends before I was ready for that title. We were on the phone talking one day, and she said, "we are friends, right?"

"Well, we're working on friendship. Don't you think friendships take time to develop?" I asked.

"I do," she said, "but I thought that we had already become friends."

What I said may have hurt her feelings, but back then I was afraid to say someone new was my friend. I feared that once she really got to know me, she would not want anything to do with me.

In spite of my fears, our friendship blossomed over the years. Jan didn't seem to mind that I had some really odd characteristics. She likes to talk on the phone, and she calls regularly. I love that and look forward to our weekly phone conversations. I also appreciate and love her forgiving spirit. She has taught me how to be forgiving, which I am so grateful for, because that has not been one of my strong suits.

I have another dear friend, Connie, who has a love for God that is actually contagious. When you talk to her you can just hear her love for God in her conversation. She can make you feel good when you are having a bad day. I don't think she has a negative bone in her body. She speaks life, and it changes my perspective almost immediately.

Darling, affectionately known as Darlene, is another old friend whom I love dearly. We were married to two brothers at one time. Ron and Mike were two of the craziest young men you could ever meet. They both came from a long line of thugs, drug dealers, addicts, alcoholics, and pimps. Two very charismatic personalities you would want to know and be around. These guys were two of the biggest con artists you would ever meet. They could charm any woman out of her panties in nanoseconds. I know Ron could; he came into my life while working at a community department store. He had me letting him drive my car, buying him weed, food, clothes, and a list that went on and on. He was one of the biggest whore mongers ever and could not resist anything wearing a skirt.

The brother Darlene married was Mike who was actually quite smart, but he could not stay out of jail to save his life. Ultimately, Darlene and I found our way out of those marriages and managed to get on with our lives with only some emotional and physical scars. I don't see or talk to Darlene much, but I love her because she was there for me in those early days when I was hurting so badly after Ron left me for Sonya. Somehow, she always knew just what to say to make me feel good about myself. Darlene has now remarried and appears to be very happy.

Ursula Murray, who just happens to be a Caucasian woman, is a good friend. Our relationship got off to a rocky start but blossomed into a beautiful friendship over the years. Ursula and her husband, Vince, have been incredibly supportive to me and my husband, and we love them dearly.

Even though my circle of friends is small, I feel blessed and fulfilled because they are in my life. I love all of my friends because I believe God gave them to me. My friends know me well, and they still like me. That means so much to me because that was always one of my greatest fears. I want to be the best friend that I can be. I am a loyal and dedicated friend, and I will do anything to help those who are close to me. Since moving to Georgia, I have missed my friends terribly, but thank God for technology that keeps us connected on a regular basis.

Amore Di Vita

"Amore Di Vita" is the name of my Professional Counseling business. The name means Love of Life in Italian. I am living my best life now. I have a real love of life today, and it is because God saw fit to give me a beautiful husband who is warm and caring. He has an amazing spirit and a deep love for our life together. We have had some amazingly fun times during our marriage.

One of our most memorable trips was during our honeymoon, when we traveled to Puerto Vallarta, Mexico. Another of our memorable trips was to Disney World, and we had a wonderful time. We also went to Sea World, and we both really enjoyed our time there. I didn't even mind all the water splashing on me.

One of our really great trips was when we traveled to Jamaica. I never dreamed I could travel to different countries, but God made it possible. I am not sure what I expected to experience in Jamaica. We stayed at a Sandals Resort in the town of Montego Bay. The Resort was absolutely beautiful. Even the Peacocks came to check it out. The sandy beach and the entertainment there were exquisite. I even got a chance to assist the Elvis impersonator during a show at the hotel one evening. I was shaking in my boots as I waited to go on the stage. My little role only consisted of handing him a rose, but I was still nervous.

During our stay in Jamaica, we toured some of the local areas, and had an opportunity to see how the locals lived. Much to my surprise, life outside of the resort was very depressed. People sold fish on street corners in order to feed their families. Once, while David was getting his nails done, the manicurist told him she would willingly give her daughter to someone who could give her a better life. I found that to be very sad.

I loved spending time with my husband and seeing parts of the world I never knew existed. I will forever remember those amazing experiences. We walked along the white sandy beaches that fronted some of the most beautiful blue water I had ever seen. The tours that took us up into the lush, green mountainsides were amazing. We ate lunch at an outside restaurant where we met some beautiful village children, who sang for us.

My husband and I have also traveled to the Bahamas on multiple occasions. Once with his family, and another time alone to enjoy ourselves. The Bahamas are beautiful, and we enjoyed being entertained there. Good food and much needed relaxation provided just what we needed to escape from our busy lives and hectic work schedules. We have been blessed to have some amazing travel experiences, and I expect we will have many more.

Not only do we love to travel, we love music, also. Jazz music is our all-time favorite, but we love rhythm and blues, gospel, country, and even some rap music. We have been fortunate enough to attend lots of wonderful Jazz concerts. While living in Michigan we often went to jazz concerts. We became fans of Bony James, a jazz saxophonist. Back in the day, Bakers Keyboard Lounge provided opportunities to enjoy jazz artists.

Many years ago, my girlfriend Marsha invited me to go with her to see Marion Meadows and Will Downing. I had not known about either of those artists at the time, but we went to downtown Detroit, on the riverfront, to a small club called The Warehouse. We had seats right up front, and we were so close we could almost touch them when they performed. I will never forget that wonderful evening. Marsha passed away a few years ago, as she lost her struggle with heart and diabetes problems. She was a beautiful person, and she had a love for life and enjoyed music so very much. Rest in peace Marsha.

We have discovered a wonderful venue here in Atlanta. Though smaller than some of the others, the Cobb Energy Center provides perfect sound quality for concerts and plays. We have seen multiple artists at this wonderful place including Norman Brown, Brian Culberson, and Jonathan Butler, to name a few. Norman Brown is a jazz guitarist, and If I close my eyes and listen closely, I can hear him playing "Come Go with Me," which is one of my favorites. Brian Culberson's "It's on Tonight" is a tune that is so sexy. It is like a mating ritual—absolutely beautiful.

There are some other nice places to hear jazz, but they are a bit further away from where we live. The Velvet Note in Alpharetta is one of those places. It is small but comfortable, and I was pleasantly surprised to discover how intimate the setting was when we took our friend "Snook" there during one of his visits.

Leaving Michigan

Several years after my husband retired from Ford Motor Company, he became obsessed with the idea of moving from Michigan to a warmer climate. I wasn't totally against moving away from Michigan, but I knew I did not want to move back to Jacksonville, Alabama. I really thought I wanted to live in Florida, and so we planned to go to Orlando and look around. We got in touch with a local realtor who showed us some new construction homes. The homes were beautiful but way too close together for my liking.

During our visit to Orlando, I discovered there was a season for the "Love Bugs." They are small insects that fly in swarms during a certain time in the summer season. They were everywhere, flying into the car as we drove along, and into our faces as we walked outside. In addition to the love Bugs, I found the heat excruciating. My bright mind concluded it only involved the area we were visiting; surely these annoying insects could not possibly be in all of Florida.

Our next trip brought us to Fort Walton Beach and Destin, Florida, smaller coastal towns in the Florida panhandle. Destin was a beautiful area and so was Fort Walton Beach. However, the traffic was pretty bad, because it had become a popular tourist destination. We spent a few days in the area just looking around, and once again, I found the heat unbearable. We went from there to Mobile, Alabama, and I can remember my sister-in-law asking me if I was all right.

I must have looked really bad, and I felt that way because the heat had gotten to me and left me tired, lethargic, and dried out.

Also, during our search to find a new location in a warmer climate, we also visited Arizona. I loved Arizona, but had we gone there we would have been too far away from everyone we knew.

The White And Black Thing

"Sometimes, I feel discriminated against, but it does not make me angry. It merely astonishes me. How can any deny themselves the pleasure of my company? It's beyond me." –Zora Neale Hurston

I know now that I was bigoted when it came to how I felt about White people. Most people are not willing to say it, but I am. I grew up in the deep south during a time when racism was perpetuated in all walks of life. Some of my earliest memories of racism are still vivid in my mind. I recall when my dad and I went into town so he could meet with one of the business owners about doing some work for him. The business was a local restaurant, and as soon as we walked inside, I started asking for a hamburger. Daddy told me I could eat when we got back home. I was persistent, as most five- or six-year-old children would be about getting something that they want. In my child's mind it was that burger.

The woman behind the counter must have overheard our conversation, because she said, "Don't worry about it, I will make her a burger." That made me so very happy though I wasn't old enough to understand that they did not serve Black people in that restaurant at that time. However, my dad clearly understood the dynamics of the day. There were still "colored" water fountains and requirements for Blacks to enter thorough the back-doors back then. Looking back, I realize my dad could have been afraid of a number of things happening because of that burger. I have often heard that when some of the restaurants started serving black people, the workers would spit in their food or worse. I can imagine that even after she made that burger, he was leery of me eating it.

As I grew older, I realized that as Black people living where we lived, and in other places, but especially where we lived, we did not have equal rights. We were forced to leave our schools and attend the all-White schools, where people hated us just for being Black. I remember that some of the teachers were really mean and did not want us there. Some of the Black students got into arguments with some of the White students who called them niggers. There were instances where the White students spit on some of the Black students.

In retrospect, I find it interesting that the Black students were not expected to defend themselves against that blatant racism. If a Black student did defend himself or herself, he or she was seen as a trouble maker or just an angry Black person. Based on my experience, there was no fairness attributed to Black people back then, and in my opinion, change has been slow, and forward motion in equality continues to be a challenge.

How I Got My Love For Shoes

My mama was beautiful despite the moles that covered her face and which she refused to have removed. In spite of the fact that she had a strong personality and at times may have discouraged people from wanting to get close to her, those of us who knew her intimately loved her deeply. She loved nice clothes and shoes. My mom had the most beautiful shapely legs, and when she put on a dress and some nice shoes, she was a "knock out." I often say I wished I had legs like hers, because mine are muscular and skinny. I could have been the cover child for the song written by the singer Joe Text, "Skinny Legs and All."

Even though we did not have a lot of money, my mother managed to purchase quality

95

shoes for me. Her motto was that "one should buy quality because it will last longer," and I embraced that idea when it comes to purchasing clothes and shoes. I love shoes and have purchased and worn some of the most beautiful footwear anyone could want. I believe my love of shoes is a legacy that my godchildren and all who know me will inherit.

When Danielle was a little girl all of her outfits that I purchased had perfectly matching shoes to go with them. My oldest Godchild Ishamia also enjoyed shoes that I purchased for her. And although she says she is not "a girly girl," I still think she loves shoes.

I have a dream of traveling to Milan, Italy, to shop for shoes one day. I hope I will be able to afford the trip and bring back lots of gorgeous Italian-made shoes.

I recently discovered the more affluent shoe styles and cost. I went into Saks Fifth Avenue and tried on shoes that I never thought I would be able to own. However, my wonderful husband opened an account and bought me the most beautiful pair of Celine of Paris boots. I am in love and can't wait to wear them.

I tried on lots of shoes while in that store, and while I am waiting on my chance to go to Italy, I will just have to appease myself by buying a pair or so every year. I know my mama is smiling in heaven as she sees me wearing these beautiful shoes. Although I imagine the ones she wears now are unsurpassed by comparison.

The Love of My Life Diagnosed With Cancer

When Doctor Faye came into the room, she greeted us with her usual bubbly attitude. "Good Morning David, Sandra," she said.

"Good morning, Doctor Faye," we both said.

She went over David's annual physical exam results and said, "David, all of your blood work looks good." She read some of the other details on a paper she held in her hand then walked over to where I was sitting and pointed to the numbers on the form.

She looked at us and asked, "What is the urologist saying about David's PSA count?"

David had a blank look on his face, so I said, "I'm not sure exactly, but why do you ask?"

She said, "I asked because his PSA levels have been continually rising since 2016, and the level is at 4.0 currently." She went on to explain what the rising levels indicated. "The urologist should be doing a biopsy at this point."

I looked at her and said, "I don't care for his urologist, and I've said that to David. Do you have another recommendation?"

She responded immediately. "Yes, there is a doctor that another of my patients uses; I will be happy to share his contact information."

As soon as we were in the car, I dialed the number of the doctor she recommended and made an appointment to meet with him. We soon discovered his office was on the other side of Atlanta, which was about an hour's drive from where we lived. That had me a little concerned, but of course I wanted my husband to have the best medical care he could receive.

When we finally arrived, I quickly assessed the inside of the office. I wanted to make sure it was clean and that the staff was professional. I thought that the office was fairly clean. When we approached the counter to check in, the person there was polite. We checked in and waited to be called back. Once inside, we were directed to an examination room where we waited to be seen.

A nurse came in and talked with us briefly. Then a Technician came in and asked more questions and stated that the doctor wanted David to have a test in the office. David agreed to have it done, and I said that I would wait outside.

"No honey," David said. "Stay here with me."

I intended to give him a little privacy, but he did not want me to leave, so I stayed.

After about an hour of questioning and waiting, the doctor came in. He was a young man of East Indian ancestry. He talked, and we both asked questions. He told us he needed to do more tests and to get the medical records from the other urologist David had been seeing.

We left there and headed home. "This is a long way to come to see a doctor," I said.

"Yes, it is pretty far," David said. As we drove along, we talked more about the doctor and the drive, and agreed that we would go to see his original specialist and tell him what Doctor Faye had said about the biopsy. I called and made an appointment to see Dr. Proctor.

On the scheduled date, we arrived at Doctor Proctor's office and waited to be called in. Once we were in the waiting room, we talked about the questions we would ask. David, in his usual kindhearted way, did not want to say anything that would upset anyone. I, on the other hand, was armed with many things I intended to tell this doctor.

"Hello David," he said and nodded at me. I thought, how odd, but I was sure his receptionist had passed along my concerns from our conversation when I made the appointment.

"I understand you have some concerns about a biopsy," He said.

I jumped right in. "Yes, we do. We met with David's Internal Medicine Doctor, who pointed out how David's PSA has been rising. She wanted to know why a biopsy had not been done."

"I don't like the way you are talking to me," Dr. Proctor shot back.

"I can ask you questions, can't I?" I responded.

"You are asking me questions that I have already given David information about."

"Well, I wasn't here when you gave him that information, and I want to know what is going on."

"You are being rude," he said.

"I'm not being any more rude than you are," I said, then added, "You are not God."

We all sat silently for a while to let things settle down. Eventually, Dr. Proctor gave us a few more details about his process and tried to defend his professionalism. At that point I was pretty much done with him. However, David just listened and took everything in. The doctor recommended continuing to treat David's urinary tract infection for a few more weeks, and then have him take another PSA Test.

I made a decision right then that I would go with David for all of his appointments with this doctor in the future. David went back for the PSA test, and the results came back still high. At this appointment the doctor stated that a biopsy should now be scheduled. It was conducted, and we scheduled a follow up appointment to get the results.

We had been waiting for a few weeks to get the results of the prostate biopsy. I could tell it was weighing heavily on David; he was quiet around the house and not talking much. This was very different for him since he loves to talk. I tried not to appear concerned, but there was no peace in my spirit about the report soon to come.

Sitting in the small doctor's examination room for about 40 minutes made me anxious. "What's going on?" I asked David.

"I don't know," he said. "How long have we been in here?"

I looked at my watch. "Forty-five minutes." I got up, opened the door, and looked out. I noticed the doctor pushing a cart in our direction.

"Thanks for opening the door for me. I apologize for the long wait," he said. "I have two in-laws in the emergency room."

"Sorry to hear that," David and I said at the same time.

The doctor talked about David's case, sort of a review. Then he said, "It saddens me to tell you this, but you have prostate cancer."

I could see his lips moving, but all I could hear was the word *cancer*. I started to cry uncontrollably. Then I heard David say, "It is going to be fine honey; I'm not going to die." His words did little to console me at that moment. I wanted to run out of that room, or curse the doctor, get mad at God—anything to make the fear and anger go away. But all I did was sit and cry, and try to take in what the doctor was saying.

He rattled off information at a rapid-fire pace. "Your prostate has a score of 4 plus 3, which equals a 7 on the scale." The news that David had prostate cancer, too, sent both of us reeling.

The drive home was quiet. I think we were both in shock. I just felt numb, though I had a million thoughts running through my mind. Most of which were rather selfish. I was thinking, what if he dies? Where will I live? Who will come see about me? Who will love me?

I was scared to death about how all of this would play out. I felt helpless and hopeless. All of that faith stuff was nowhere to be found. Nothing made sense anymore. Life was no longer as it had been for the 20 plus years I had been with my wonderful husband. I thought about how God is in control of life and death, and maybe this is my husband's time.

I could barely control the thoughts that kept flooding my mind. The emptiness that was growing inside of me was familiar. I remembered feeling those thoughts and emotions when my Mama was diagnosed with cancer many years ago. I thought, I cannot go through this again with someone I love. The tears fell down my face, and I had no thoughts of how to handle everything I felt. I didn't want to talk to God. If He was in control, nothing I could say would make any difference.

Not only were we trying to figure out what the next steps were going to be, we had to attend to the pain from David's Saitic nerve condition. He had been in pain for about a week, and it was not getting any better. I called his orthopedic doctor and asked her what we should do. She said to come into her office on Monday. This was Saturday, and we were thinking what we could do for the pain until we saw her on Monday.

I realized that my husband's body was under attack. We had received the news of his cancer diagnosis, and this new onset of pain was overwhelming him. I knew talking to my friends, his friends, or his family was not the answer. I had no answers. I could not help him, which forced me to talk to God.

"God," I prayed, "David is one of your best representatives on earth. He loves deeply, forgives easily, and shows kindness to everyone he comes in contact with. You need him in the earth. Please don't take him yet. Let him stay and continue to be an example of your character in the world."

I prayed hard. I didn't know if I believed God was listening or if he heard anything that I said. I just knew He was my only hope.

The next few weeks were filled with doctor's appointments and more assessments. David had a CAT scan and a bone scan. He went to see his orthopedic doctor, who sent him to see a pain management doctor, who ordered an MRI.

I wanted to just cry all the time. The tears came and they made me feel better for a moment, but I became convinced that they were not helping at all. I changed how I felt about what was happening. I allowed David to decide who would be told about his cancer diagnosis. I told my friend Jan who had some consoling words to say. However, it did not do much for how I felt. I told our pastors, and Reverend Joel came to visit David. I was happy about that and impressed at the same time.

There have been pastors with much smaller congregations, who have outright said they do not visit their parishioner's in their homes. But here was a man of God who came to our home to visit my husband. He and one of the other ministers came to visit with David and they went out and had lunch together. I will be forever grateful for that kind act. My heart is still breaking for my beautiful man of God, but his diagnosis has allowed me to see Christ more clearly.

Angels Are Real

I now understand that my husband is an angel sent from God. I don't know what angels' roles involve other than following God closely and carrying out His directions on Earth. I suppose angels sometimes have short stays on Earth. Now that I know he is an angel, I will value my time with him as even more precious. I don't know how much that time is, but whatever it is I will cherish it dearly. I may be the first to die, but because I don't have those answers, I will love him even more deeply.

David's Major Surgery

It had taken a few months, but finally all the pre-operative appointments had been made and kept. The day David would have his prostate removed arrived. I was scared to death, because even though I knew God was in charge, I desperately wanted my husband to be all right. He had been a trooper through all that happened. I, on the other hand, had my moments and my emotional melt-downs.

I had many conversations with God throughout that process. I questioned Him about why this would happen to my wonderful husband. I informed God that David was one of His best representatives on earth, as if He needed to be informed. I told God that He needed David to live a long time, because people like myself need his example to keep us doing the right thing. I said to God that David loves easily and forgives quickly, and that I want to learn how to do that.

I would have been by myself during the surgery, but Daryl Sims came to sit with me. Daryl is a part of our extended family—he, and his wife Stacy and their little daughter Elizabeth. Daryl is a general contractor and owns his own business. He has not been in business that long and is still building his clientele. The fact that he took the time to be with me and leave his business unattended makes it even more special. Not only did he come to sit with me, he actually talked to me while we waited. I will forever be appreciative for his love and concern.

My Husband Beat Cancer

Through God's grace and mercy, my husband is cancer free today. David finished all of his bio physical therapy and is doing great. He has even started walking again. He is an amazing man who loves everyone so deeply. He had to go for his PSA test, and we were a little concerned, but it came back negative. When we went to see Dr. Rosenfeld, a gastroenterologist and prostate cancer specialist, he stated that all of David's tests came back showing great results.

It has been almost three years now since David was diagnosed with prostate cancer. He has had all of his follow-up testing, and all results continue to show that he does not have any cancer in his body. We are so grateful to God for sparing his life, and we don't take it for granted. We understand now that life is a gift to be loved and enjoyed to the fullest, because tomorrow is not guaranteed. We are so grateful that God saw fit to deliver him from this deadly disease.

I Am Not Empty Or Barren, I Am Complete

When I think about babies today, I think they are so cute, and I love to hold them and play with their fat cheeks. I reminisce about what it would have been like to give birth to my own, but I am no longer consumed with the fact that I was unable to give birth. I am more consumed with the fact that God saw fit to give me babies to love and let me experience what diaper changing and baby bottles are all about. Not as much fun as I thought it would be actually, but a great experience none the less. I now know that *experiencing the pain and agony involved with childbirth is not the only characteristic of being a woman that defines me today.*

If you are a woman who has never been able to give birth and feel you have been cheated by life, I would tell you, life can be cruel and unfair, and society is even more cruel. However, God is bigger and better than all of the unfairness in the world. Allow Him to heal you from the inside out, starting with your broken heart. Know that your self-worth and value is not determined by how many babies you give birth to. Remember that You are wonderfully made in God's own image. The fact that you have not been able to have babies is no surprise to God; he knew your destiny when He formed you in your mother's womb.

There are lots of babies just waiting to be loved, if you can find it in your heart to show them that love. That love will be returned a hundredfold. I thought I was just doing God's work when I reached out to help a teen mother and her baby. I had no idea how much their loving me back would impact my life.

So, my recommendation to women who struggle with infertility is to stop beating up on yourself for something you cannot control, and let God fill you with the joy and happiness that only He can provide.

Michigan Is The Place I Choose To Call Home

I often think about moving back to Michigan, because the majority of my life's happy times occurred while I lived there. Not only are my friends and my babies there, but many of my wonderful memories are there as well. I am slowly making new memories with my husband in Georgia. Making new friends for me has been tough. I suppose I still fear the idea of letting someone get to know who I really am.

You might ask what was so great about Michigan? For me it represented a fresh start after all of the pain and misery I had experienced in Alabama. It was refreshing, and I was happy to be there. I was excited about all the possibilities that lay ahead of me.

I remember waking up after being in Michigan about three months to find snow that was about three feet deep. I had never seen anything so beautiful. I went outside and walked in the snow. I watched the flakes fall from the sky. I fell in love with the snow from the very beginning, and I am in love with it even now. Fresh fallen snow is one of the many things I miss most. Christmas in Georgia is quite different from Christmas in Michigan. At Christmas time in Michigan the snow on the trees is postcard perfect.

Adjusting to Michigan was tough for me in the beginning. I lost weight even though I was already really skinny. As time passed, I gained the weight back and settled into my new life.

Forgiveness Equals Freedom And Happiness

I am not confused about who I am anymore. I recognize today that the God I serve does not make junk regardless of the situation one is born into. I can say without any apprehension that I am a wonderful mother figure, wife, and one of the most loyal and dedicated friends anyone could have. Through God's amazing grace, my life is beautiful and fulfilled. I recognize that I am complete and whole and not the broken, damaged person I once thought I was. "For I will forgive their wickedness and will remember their sins no more." Hebrews 8:12

I forgive all the people for all of the mean and hateful things they said and did to me as an innocent child. George and James Green, now dead and gone, are at the top of my list. I forgive the people who continue to see me as being beneath them because of their ignorance and inability to show love. I pray for them now because I recognize how sad and miserable are the lives they must live. I forgive Fannie Mae for her decision to not have any contact with me or mama for years. I understand now that her life was also hard and sad.

I am blessed by God, and in spite of my tough beginnings, my life has turned out to be amazing. I have wonderful friends, people who love me dearly. I wish everyone who played a negative role in my life all the best that life has to offer them. I pray that God will show them how to love more deeply.

I am grateful to all the women with whom I attempted to develop relationships, even those who were not interested in being my friend. I recognize now that they were not a part of my destiny. Most of all, I forgive myself for all of the unkind thoughts I have had about myself.

God knows just what needs to be done in our lives, and if we allow Him to do His perfect work, we can stop hurting and live happy, productive lives. God has been so good to me that wasting anymore of my wonderful life even thinking about past hurts would be useless.

I am all about forgiveness today, because more important than anything anyone could say or do is how God's love makes up for all the disappointments and struggles that ever occurred. I recognize that in this world everyone will experience suffering and pain. I have decided that while I have breath in my body, I choose to love and enjoy my life.

No, I didn't have my birth mother or my birth father in my life growing up, but I had an amazing mother and father in Dora and Sam, and I want to think that I have made them more than proud. I love you, Mommy and Daddy; continue to rest in Jesus's arms.

I want to thank my husband David, who I call "Honey Pie," for loving the shattered and unsure Sandra and helping her heal and become the whole woman she is today. Thank you, Honey Pie, for encouraging me each and every day to see the brighter side of life. You really are my knight in shining armor.

Like many people, I continue to struggle with depression and anxiety, but it is much more manageable now. I suppose it is because I have learned to allow God to help me rise above it all, and see my life as he would have me see it, which is beautiful. I guess one could say I have discovered my *Amore Di Vita*, which is Italian for love of life. I soar on God's love and angel's wings today, and even in down moments I feel my angels lifting me up so I can experience life in a more beautiful way.

To all the women who are hurting for whatever reason, please allow God to be your best friend or family until He sends people just for you. He did it for me, and He can do it for you.

For those women struggling with infertility, allow God to send babies for you to love in whatever manner He chooses, and your life will forever be changed.

About the Author

Sandra Pugh-Monroe was born and raised in rural Alabama. Sandra was a very bright child and grew up in a home with a mother and a father who loved her with all the love they knew to give. From a young age, Sandra faced rejection and disappointment from some family members who should have shown her love. Sandra also experienced multiple forms of prejudice and blatant racism from the local white establishment where she grew up. The ultimate rejection would come as her womanhood would be defined by her inability to bear children. After moving to Michigan as a young woman, she encountered still more difficulties and stilted attitudes regarding womanhood and childbearing. Unwilling to accept the conventional wisdom, Sandra pursued an educational path, renewed her faith, and allowed God to define her life. Along the way, she met her loving husband, David Pugh, and have been happily married for 23 years. Now a licensed therapist, Sandra J. Pugh shares her life story as both an object lesson and a social commentary.

Made in the USA
Columbia, SC
16 November 2021

49069676R00063